THE AMERICAN POLITICAL EXPERIENCE:
WHAT IS THE KEY?

PROBLEMS IN POLITICAL SCIENCE
under the editorial direction of NEAL RIEMER, *University of Wisconsin-Milwaukee*

WESTERN EUROPE: WHAT PATH TO INTEGRATION?
edited by CAROL EDLER BAUMANN, *University of Wisconsin-Milwaukee*

THE REPRESENTATIVE: TRUSTEE? DELEGATE? PARTISAN? POLITICO?
edited by NEAL RIEMER, *University of Wisconsin-Milwaukee*

FREE SPEECH AND POLITICAL PROTEST
edited by MARVIN SUMMERS, *University of Wisconsin-Milwaukee*

THE AMERICAN POLITICAL EXPERIENCE: WHAT IS THE KEY?
edited by EDWARD HANDLER, *Babson Institute*

THE CENTRAL INTELLIGENCE AGENCY: PROBLEMS OF SECRECY IN A DEMOCRACY
edited by YOUNG HUM KIM, *California Western University-USIU*

LIBERALIZATION IN THE USSR: FACADE OR REALITY?
edited by D. RICHARD LITTLE, *Northern Illinois University*

OTHER VOLUMES IN PREPARATION

The American Political Experience:

WHAT IS THE KEY?

EDITED WITH AN INTRODUCTION BY
Edward Handler
Babson Institute

D. C. Heath and Company
A DIVISION OF RAYTHEON EDUCATION COMPANY
LEXINGTON, MASSACHUSETTS

FOR REBECCA, DEBORAH, AND JONATHAN

Library of Congress Card Number: 68–8048

Table of Contents

21020

The Clash of Ideas

CONFLICT OR CONSENSUS

. . . our history has *not* been *dis*continuous, has not been punctuated by the kind of internal struggles which have marked the history of most of the countries of western Europe. . . .

—DANIEL J. BOORSTIN

The argument over whether we should "stress" solidarity or conflict in American politics misleads us by advancing a false set of alternatives.

—LOUIS HARTZ

Whoever supposes . . . that American politics has been nothing more than a moving consensus, a sort of national Rotary Club luncheon, has not sufficiently reflected on the regularity of intense conflict, crisis, and violence in American history.

—ROBERT A. DAHL

ENVIRONMENT OR INHERITANCE

These democratic attitudes were not carried to the New World on the *Susan Constant* and the *Mayflower*. They were a product of the turbulent social scene created by the westering urge of the pioneers.

—RAY ALLEN BILLINGTON

The emigrants who fixed themselves on the shores of America in the beginning of the seventeenth century severed the democratic principle from all the principles which repressed it in the old communities of Europe, and transplanted it unalloyed to the New World. . . .

I see the destiny of America embodied in the first Puritan who landed on those shores. . . .

—ALEXIS DE TOCQUEVILLE

RELEVANCE OR UNIQUENESS

The United States may properly claim the title of the first new nation. . . . So perhaps [it] can contribute more than money to the latter-day ones; perhaps its development can give us some clues as to how revolutionary equalitarianism and populist values may eventually become incorporated into a stable nonauthoritarian polity.

—SEYMOUR M. LIPSET

The phrase "new nation" . . . misses crucial differences between the American experience and those of the contemporary modernizing countries. The latter are . . . more accurately described . . . [as] "Old Societies and New States." America, on the other hand, was historically a new society but an old state.

—SAMUEL P. HUNTINGTON

PLURALISTIC DIVERSITY OR ELITE DOMINANCE

The fundamental axiom in the theory and practice of American pluralism is, I believe, this: Instead of a single center of sovereign power there must be multiple centers of power, none of which is or can be wholly sovereign.

—ROBERT A. DAHL

. . . at the top there has emerged an elite whose power probably exceeds that of any small group of men in world history.

—C. WRIGHT MILLS

. . . there has been a genuine growth of autonomous governmental power . . . and . . . one major aspect of this has been relatively effective control of the business system.

—TALCOTT PARSONS

Introduction

Interpretations of American politics are as old as the Republic. Indeed there is warrant for saying that they even antedate the Republic. Franklin and Adams in Paris in the years of the War of Independence were astonished to encounter a number of French intellectuals eagerly engaged in studying the new revolutionary state constitutions and concocting explanations of their liberal features. Even before the adoption of the federal Constitution the advance guard had appeared of a seemingly endless legion of foreign observers who, from Brissot de Warville to Brogan, were prompted by attraction or repulsion, but in any case fascination, to formulate hypotheses intended to unlock the secrets of American political life.

Americans themselves have not lagged far behind these foreign observers in producing synoptic views of their own politics. The result has been the accumulation throughout our history of a variety of unifying visions of the meaning underlying American political thought and practice. They have ranged from Jefferson's idea that American institutions recaptured the essentials of the ancient Saxon constitution—a view that reverberates in Woodrow Wilson's statement that, politically speaking, Americans were "living an old life under new conditions"—all the way to Harold Laski's Marxist dictum that American democracy has been essentially "a democracy of the middle-class, which assumes, though it does not announce, the authority of wealth," and which is careful not to "jeopardize the claims that men of property invariably put forward as the boundaries beyond which democracy may not pass."

Although duly acknowledging a long tradition of interpretation, this volume focuses, with one significant exception, upon recent unifying visions of American politics. It brings together a group of writings by students of American political thought and institutions, done largely since 1945 and concerned with comprehensive analysis of the American political experience. Each author concentrates his

1

attention upon one leading question: *What is the key to the mysteries of American politics?* Each formulates or offers a critique of some major hypothesis about the distinctive features of American political behavior, values, and institutions.

Understandably, although such efforts to encompass in theoretical constructions the rich phenomena of American politics coincide in many particulars, they often clash fundamentally. In this conflict of standpoints one may discern, in fact, certain patterns of recurrent controversy, which will be explored in this book. These disagreements, clustering around a number of issues central to the interpretation of American politics, may be stated in terms of a set of polarities, as follows: (1) Is American politics dominantly the reflection of conflict or consensus, of periodically sharp social and ideological struggles, or of the social solidarity, moral unity, and down-to-earth pragmatism peculiar to the American people? (2) Which is the primary shaping force in American politics— environment or inheritance? (3) How atypical is American political experience? Is it more meaningfully interpreted as "exceptional" or like the political experience of other societies? Is the American polity a model for others, or is it so unique as to render its study irrelevant to them? (4) Is it in elite dominance or in pluralistic diversity that one finds the ultimate reality of American politics?

Conflict or Consensus

In his classic *Democracy in America,* from which the opening selection of Part I is taken, Alexis de Tocqueville described the remarkable ideological and social homogeneity which he saw underpinning American political life. The essential meaning that he attached to this celebrated unifying concept, "equality of condition," was that in America "men differ but little from each other." Viewing America from the vantage point of France's fierce ideological dissensions and unresolved social struggles, he was struck particularly by the substantial concurrence of Americans in a certain number of opinions, tastes, and propensities which were seemingly beyond criticism. Americans did not, like the French, have to dispossess the aristocratic principle by violent means. The political community was therefore not rent into two groups—those exhibiting the "rancorous passions" of men who have had to shake off a long-established authority, and those animated by bitter regret over the passing of their power.

Not only possessed of an unerring eye for the bonds of community among Americans, Tocqueville was also far too sagacious and catholic an observer to miss the basic sources of cleavage in American society. He saw in the march of industrialism the materials for the reemergence of a possibly permanent social inequality; he was on the whole pessimistic about the ability of the federal union to accommodate the potentially explosive pressures of a growing regional differentiation; he took note gravely of the inherent incompatibility between the situation of black men and a basic equality of condition more completely realized than elsewhere in the Western world. Nevertheless, Tocqueville's enumeration of multiple cleavages was ultimately a qualification of a thesis whose main drift was the minimization of conflict.

Both the Boorstin and Hartz analyses are Tocquevillean in derivation and dominantly consensual in emphasis. For Daniel J. Boorstin in his *The Genius of American Politics* it is axiomatic that in American politics there has been relatively little disagreement on ends, that the same political institutions have persisted throughout the national existence, and that our history has not been punctuated by the kind of internal social struggles that have marked the history of Europe. He feels that the national consciousness has been permeated by a sense of "givenness," by an implicit assumption of the validity of its political norms, and he finds the American system the supreme example of anti-ideological politics. Without the European preoccupation with "political dogma," Americans have reaped the rewards of a marvelous and unashamed practicality; in Boorstin's opinion, this is why their politicians have been free to exercise great flexibility and an experimental attitude in the solution of problems.

Louis Hartz, in his influential *The Liberal Tradition in America* also stresses institutional continuity, the absence of significant political thought, and unanimity of basic political values in American politics. But he differs from Boorstin in his derivation of these attributes, and he is less reconciled to some of their consequences. Although in discussing some historic American conflict situations he emphasizes their "phantom" nature—in his view their intensity was more rhetorical than real—he insists that he does not mean to deny the actuality of conflict in American politics. He does not disagree with the notion that adherents of the same ideology may quarrel violently about its application. However, the special quality and meaning of American political conflicts are missed, he argues, if it is not understood that, unlike the typical experience of some key European countries, these conflicts were fought out in the context of a single dominant ideology.

For Hartz the key to American political development is that America missed the ideological diversity which arose from European feudalism. Only one European ideology—liberalism—was transplanted here, to develop in isolation from competing ideologies. Genuine conservatism, reaction, and socialism all languished in the American environment. In Hartz's opinion, the impression that Americans have had an anti-ideological politics is the result not of the absence of ideology on the American political scene but of the overwhelming presence of a single one, and the vaunted pragmatism of American politicians is to be traced to their fear of appearing to challenge the "deafening" liberal consensus. Without the experience of ideological diversity, the United States may have missed the conflicts of Europe, but, according to Hartz, some less happy results have been the "mindlessness" peculiar to American politics, the major internal difficulties in tolerating dissent, and, especially since 1945, the increasing foreign relations problem of learning to adjust to an external environment richly endowed with precisely the ideological diversity never encountered directly at home.

In his essay on the "cult of consensus" John Higham offers a critique of Boorstin and Hartz. As an intellectual historian, he is occupied primarily with the question of why they view American politics as they do. He sees Boorstin and Hartz repudiating the perspectives of an earlier generation of scholars, who, writing as Progressives in an age of reform, tended to paint America "in the broad hues of conflict." Under external threat, however, a society is prone to become more concerned with the elements that bind it together. Higham maintains that the challenge of revolutionary totalitarianism after 1945 produced a mood of conservative satisfaction with American politics that led to a new emphasis—as appears in Boorstin and Hartz—on its specifically non-European aspects: continuity, stability, and ideological consensus.

The foundation of Higham's analysis is the assumption that changes in the interpretation of American political life will reflect changes in the political environment. In these terms a "thaw" in the cold war and the sharpening of conflicts within the country might be expected to shift the emphasis of interpretation once again. It is instructive in this regard to note that there is scarcely any reflection of the civil rights struggle in Boorstin's and Hartz's analysis, their work having appeared when cold-war fever was most intense and the "new abolitionism" only beginning to take shape.

In the first of two excerpts from his *Pluralist Democracy in the United States,* Robert A. Dahl appears highly responsive to the new context of revived domestic conflict. Thus he is critical of what he takes to be an obsessive concern with the value of stability in contemporary American political science, and he rejects the notion that American politics has been nothing more than a "moving consensus." He points out that since the 1790's American political life has undergone roughly every generation a conflict of extreme severity. (The historical documentation of this thesis centers on a number of situations which for Hartz illustrate the "phantom" nature of American political struggles.) Dahl distinguishes between moderate and severe conflicts, and offers the arresting hypothesis that certain attributes of the American system of constitutional and social pluralism render it highly effective in absorbing moderate conflicts but possibly incapacitate it for dealing effectively with really severe conflicts.

Environment or Inheritance

The frontier thesis, first announced by Frederick Jackson Turner in 1893, was for many decades the most widely accepted single interpretation of American political development. Turner felt that natural conditions—the pioneer's encounter with the wilderness and the enticement of the free land in the West—were the primary influences in shaping American democracy. Subjected to criticism, especially in the 1930's and 1940's, the frontier thesis has fallen more recently into disrepute. But it remains the most important example of one possible major approach to the interpretation of American politics—environmental determinism.

In Ray Allen Billington, Turner continues to have an indefatigable and skillful champion. Billington reaffirms Turner's thesis with qualifications to take account of criticism. He argues that if three centuries of frontiering were not responsible for the general American devotion to democracy, they *were* responsible for the differences between American democracy and European democracy. He assembles evidence to show that if the Westerners did not innovate the democratic practices peculiar to Americans, they did strengthen them immensely.

At first glance a number of Tocqueville's observations in the second selection from *Democracy in America* place him in the environmentalist camp, and indeed Neo-Turnerians like Billington customarily cite him as a precursor of their master. What could be more conclusive, apparently, than Tocqueville's tribute to the magnificence of the North American natural setting: "Nature herself favors the cause of the people"? But such statements must be understood in the context of his final reflection that the customs or manners of the Americans (rooted in their Old World historical and cultural inheritance, and *not* in their racial genes, for Tocqueville was an opponent of racial explanations of politics) contributed more to the democratic republic than did the physical circumstances of the country. He found the origins of the equality of condition from which the democratic republic ultimately stemmed in the "point of departure" of the first settlers. As he remarked in a suggestive hyperbole, the whole history of the nation was embodied, as it were, in the original Puritans who came ashore. Tocqueville, moreover, through the force of the comparative method which he habitually brought to bear upon his data, anticipated one of the criticisms later to be made of the frontier thesis: There were other frontiers in the New World (he cites French Canada and Latin America), but in none of these was there a democratic result.

In *People of Plenty* David Potter maintains a qualified and even ambiguous environmentalist position and criticizes what he regards as the crude geographical determinism of Turner and his followers. For Potter, the chief factor conditioning American politics has been our unprecedented material abundance. He traces the special traits of American democracy to the pervasive influence of an economic surplus, which has had the effects of muting conflict, easing the problems of attaining social justice, and rendering class struggle superfluous. (As a result, Potter, as much as Boorstin or Hartz, views American politics in consensualist terms, although finding the basis for consensus in a quite different single-factor analysis.) Turner's frontier, according to Potter, is merely one of the contexts in which economic abundance occurred.

Potter also feels that Turner dwelt too exclusively on the properties of the primary or physical environment. He is certain that American democracy was indelibly stamped with the imprint of economic abundance, but he is hesitant to assign either primary or secondary environment the major influence in creating that abundance: his final conclusion is that a mutual interaction was required. In the context of his discussion Potter defines secondary environment as essentially those cultural traits and dispositions which enabled Americans to exploit with vigor the resources of the physical environment. Were such traits and dispositions produced by the stimulus of the physical environment itself, or were they a part of the cultural inheritance carried from Europe by key groups of settlers? Potter would seem to lean toward the first alternative.

In the analysis of Louis Hartz (see the excerpt from *The Liberal Tradition in America* in Part I) an environmentalism denied entrance through the front door gains admission through a back entry. The American political experience represents for Hartz the inevitable unfolding of a single ideological framework. He unequivocally supports the case for the priority of "idea" and inheritance over environment, yet he feels compelled to take notice of the material setting, however fleetingly. He quotes with approval the telling but environmentalist aphorism of William Graham Sumner: "We have not made America, America has made us." Or, as Hartz puts it himself, the liberal idea in America was "peculiarly fortified by the riches of a rich land." His opinion is that the environment by itself did not produce the liberal society, but it helped to explain the remarkable ease of the liberal triumph.

The environmentalist emphasis, which in Hartz is clearly subsidiary, dominates the analysis of Boorstin. (Here we find a sharp difference between two interpretations of American politics that are often regarded as substantially similar.) The student who has read the excerpt from *The Genius of American Politics* in Part I will not have failed to notice Boorstin's appeal to the "virtues of the land." In his view that American values are "given by the landscape," there is more than an echo of Turner's emphasis on the transforming power of the frontier. Furthermore, Boorstin maintains that the baggage of "idea" that the settlers brought with them often proved irrelevant, that their cultural inheritance had constantly to be unlearned. The continuously experienced need for adaptation to the requirements of the new environment nurtured the pragmatic, anti-ideological bent of the Americans.

Relevance or Uniqueness

The proliferation of new nations in Asia and Africa has stimulated a new field of inquiry in the social sciences—the study of development. A number of scholars, prominent among them Seymour Lipset, have suggested that the United States in its early national period, as the first major colony successfully to revolt against imperial rule, presents many analogies to the contemporary modernizing countries.

In this period America had to deal with major political problems like the ones facing new nations today. Lipset adopts a method developed by the German sociologist Max Weber to isolate the distinctive features of a given society. Weber specified key historical situations whose outcome established certain values and predispositions which in turn determined later events. Using this approach, Lipset examines the formative years of the Republic and finds the source of characteristic American political values in the decisions and choices then made to resolve a number of critical problems, like the need to create a new legitimate authority and to establish national identity.

In Samuel Huntington's opinion, the effort to make connections between what is happening in Asia and Africa in the twentieth century and what happened in the United States in the eighteenth century can "only contribute to monstrous misunderstandings of both historical experiences." Huntington develops a picture of the American system as an example of "imperfect modernization." He points out that since the principal elements of the sixteenth-century English "Tudor polity" were exported to the New World and were given new life at precisely the time when they were abandoned in the home country, America was a new society but an old state. Now it represents the acme of modernity in economic and social organization, but its polity remains quaintly antique. In Huntington's opinion, because the obstacles to economic and social modernization found in old societies did not exist in America, "modernization" in the political sphere could be incomplete.

In raising the issue of whether the United States in the eighteenth century was significantly similar to modern emerging countries, Lipset and Huntington are really dealing with one aspect of the larger problem of the relevance of American political experience— a problem central to the interpretation of American politics and as such touched on by several of the authors represented in this volume. Thus for Boorstin American development has been unique, to the point where we have neither institutions nor a theory of government to offer others. In his analysis, American political experience demonstrates instead the wisdom of allowing institutions to develop according to the needs of their own particular environments and differing historical inheritances. None of the other authors who touch upon this issue pushes the thesis of uniqueness so far. Even Huntington, who concludes that the American polity is irrelevant to modernizing countries, ends with the qualification that for societies that have accomplished modernization the American pattern of "dispersed and relaxed political institutions" is likely to become more applicable.

Hartz' interpretation of America as a uniquely nonfeudal society implies agreement with Huntington that its experience must be particularly irrelevant to traditional societies seeking to modernize themselves; nevertheless it must be remembered that Hartz always views America in a comparative perspective—as a variant and an extension of Europe. He affirms that "ultimately, . . . for all of the magical chemistry of American liberal society, we are dealing with social [and ideological] materials common to the Western world."

Tocqueville disclaimed intention to recommend the laws of the United States for imitation by others, because he considered that it would be a tragedy for liberty to assume everywhere the same form. But he saw the equality of condition already attained by the Americans as the coming fate of all peoples, and he took heart from their demonstration that liberty was compatible with equality. For Tocqueville there were both unique and universal elements in the political experience of the Americans.

The controversy about the uniqueness of the American political experience, long a vital one in the quest for American self-understanding, has become fraught with serious implications for American foreign policy under the impact of the extraordinary world prominence of the United States since 1945. As America has come to exert more weight in world affairs (either by decision or default of decision), what Americans believe about the relevance of their own political experience contributes inescapably to setting directions for the exercise of their influence abroad.

Pluralistic Diversity or Elite Dominance

John Fischer, following the lead of Peter Drucker, locates in the political philosophy of John C. Calhoun the clue to what really happens in American politics. According to the Neo-Calhounite version of pluralism, the central problem of politics in America has been to hold together a "frightening diversity" of sections, races, religions, and economic groups, and to adjust the tensions between them. The problem is resolved through the principle of the concurrent majority, which requires in practice "unanimous agreement by all the interested parties," before a given decision is made. According to Fischer, power in the American system of government is so dispersed that no single interest can win an entire domination over it. Because every group can exercise a "veto" over policies that vitally affect it, decision-making in American politics consists primarily of subtle, complex, and unceasing processes of negotiation. Conciliation and compromise are the hallmarks of American politics. Fischer's interpretation emphasizes the uniqueness of American politics, its anti-ideological bent, and its primary need to cope with heterogeneity and conflict.

Richard Current grants only a superficial plausibility at best to the Neo-Calhounite position. Throughout our history different combinations of interests have dominated decision-making and have overridden other interests. The system does not appease every minority; some are consistently overlooked. Decisions are not reached on the basis of unanimity; instead, working majorities are constructed through combination of several, but not all, interests. Current insists that majoritarianism is the guiding element in American politics, that the "veto group" model neither describes accurately the theory or practice of the present nor faithfully reflects the teachings of Calhoun.

A pluralist approach to American politics with nuances and emphases rather different from those of Neo-Calhounism appears in the second selection from Robert Dahl. Constitutionally the American system is pluralist, according to Dahl, because instead of a single unified center of decision it provides multiple and competing centers, none of which is wholly sovereign. Socially the American system is pluralist because no single organized interest group can control all the centers of power. Dahl differs from Current and is closer to the position of Fischer in his stress upon the numerous ways in which the rule of majorities is qualified in the American system. He finds that the emergence of a clear-cut majority will, with incontrovertible legitimacy and the power to implement its program, is a rarity in American politics. Minorities are provided with a variety of fortified positions from which to delay or even block policies seen as unfriendly to them. As Dahl sees it, American politics places a premium on taming power and limiting coercion, and permits change ordinarily only on the basis of very widely shared agreement. He reasons, therefore, that "minorities rule," rather than simple majoritarianism, is normally the key to American politics. If this is Dahl's version of the pluralist interpretation, how can it be said to differ from Fischer's? Principally in his observations (1) that influence over decisions is distributed highly unevenly among groups; (2) that there are groups which because of inactivity or lack of community legitimacy have no voice and can be excluded from the game; and (3) that the influence of even active and legitimate groups may consist of the ability effectively to be heard on matters of concern, but that such influence cannot be said to extend—as the Neo-Calhounite seems to maintain—to an *invariable* power of veto over decisions distasteful to them.

For C. Wright Mills the pluralist analyses are part of the folk-lore of how American democracy works. They have the ideological function of legitimizing or concealing the realities of the structure of power in the United States. At most they describe the American "system of power" at its "middle levels," not where the "big decisions" of national and international life are made. Mills revives the "elite dominance model," which in a variety of forms, Progressive, Marxist, or Veblenian, has had a flourishing life in the tradition of interpreting American politics. Mills contends that in contrast to the supposed pluralism of American society there has developed an unprecedented concentration of power in the hands of a small, relatively integrated business-military-political elite, which operates substantially outside the context of the historic restraints of our society. The political segment of this elite, moreover, is not autonomous, but subordinate to the business and military segments.

Talcott Parsons denies or qualifies Mills' major propositions: from his standpoint, Mills has not sustained his case that "the power structure impinging directly on American government is in [the] process of crystallizing into a top business-military coalition with a much weaker political 'junior partner' whose main function . . . is, by manipulation of the mass media and the political process, . . . to keep the great majority of Americans from protesting too loudly or even awakening to what allegedly is 'really' going on." Parsons argues that the power wielded in society by the business elite is more limited than Mills describes; that there has been a growth, not a decline, of autonomous governmental power which is able to exert genuine control over the business system; and that, while the prominence of the military has increased, it continues firmly subject to civilian authority. Essentially Parsons finds that the pluralism of group life in America is still intact; that, although the power of some other components of American society has grown, so has that of government; and that the government is not a "captive," but remains broadly responsive to a wide variety of groups—ultimately, to popular control.

However many controversies the authors in this volume present, they are nevertheless at one in at least three important respects. Responding in varying degrees to the onrush of forces that have overwhelmed traditional American insularity, they are in general more aware than the preceding generation of social scientists of the advantages in comparing American politics to the political experience of other societies, both European and non-European. Furthermore, their empirical analyses are interwoven closely with value judgments. On one level, they seek to comprehend the underlying reality of American politics. But they do more. Implicitly or explicitly, they state preferences and express value attitudes about the reality they perceive. (Robert Dahl tells us not only that compromise is native to American politics but also that some of our great compromises were morally reprehensible.) The work of these social scientists illustrates that both empirical and normative considerations are inescapably part of the study of politics. Finally, it ought to be noted that the interpretations these writers offer are dominantly single-factor: They do not break with the long tradition of explaining American politics in terms of the operation of some one major determinant. The student who notices this feature of their work will be prompted undoubtedly to consider whether any unifying vision by itself can comprehend the whole range of American politics or whether one must frankly say that our political system has always been—or has become—too elusive and intricate to admit of a single-factor interpretation. But even if this be admitted, there remains still the question: Which interpretation seems relatively most efficient in ordering the phenomena of American politics? Which provides the best available key to the mysteries of American politics?

I Conflict or Consensus

ALEXIS DE TOCQUEVILLE
Equality of Condition

Alexis de Tocqueville, the nineteenth-century French political theorist and statesman, made a journey to the United States in 1831 to study penitentiary systems. The issue of these travels was Democracy in America *(1835–1840), a volume remarkable for its penetration and power of generalization, and still holding its place as probably the most important single work by a foreigner broadly interpreting American politics and society. Tocqueville's other major work,* The Old Regime and the Revolution *(1856), is a noteworthy contribution to the understanding of the French Revolution and to the general theory of revolution. The following excerpts from* Democracy in America *introduce the organizing concept of the work and examine some sources of consensus in American life.*

AMONG THE NOVEL OBJECTS that attracted my attention during my stay in the United States, nothing struck me more forcibly than the general equality of conditions. I readily discovered the prodigious influence which this primary fact exercises on the whole course of society, by giving a certain direction to public opinion, and a certain tenor to the laws; by imparting new maxims to the governing powers, and peculiar habits to the governed.

I speedily perceived that the influence of this fact extends far beyond the political character and the laws of the country, and that it has no less empire over civil society than over the government; it creates opinions, engenders sentiments, suggests the ordinary practices of life, and modifies whatever it does not produce.

The more I advanced in the study of American society, the more I perceived that the equality of conditions is the fundamental fact

From Alexis de Tocqueville, *Democracy in America,* I, 11–12, 47–49, 52–56; II, 107–108, 317–319. New York: J. and H. G. Langley, 1841. Trans. by Henry Reeve.

from which all others seem to be derived, and the central point at which all my observations constantly terminated. . . .

The emigrants who fixed themselves on the shores of America in the beginning of the seventeenth century, severed the democratic principle from all the principles which repressed it in the old communities of Europe, and transplanted it unalloyed to the New World. It has there been allowed to spread in perfect freedom, and to put forth its consequences in the laws by influencing the manners of the country.

*   *   *

The Striking Characteristic of the Social Condition of the Anglo-Americans Is Its Essential Democracy

Many important observations suggest themselves upon the social condition of the Anglo-Americans; but there is one which takes precedence of all the rest. The social condition of the Americans is eminently democratic; this was its character at the foundation of the colonies, and is still more strongly marked at the present day.

I have stated . . . that great equality existed among the emigrants who settled on the shores of New England. The germ of aristocracy was never planted in that part of the Union. The only influence which obtained there was that of intellect; the people were used to reverence certain names as the emblems of knowledge and virtue. Some of their fellow-citizens acquired a power over the rest which might truly have been called aristocratic, if it had been capable of invariable transmission from father to son.

This was the state of things to the east of the Hudson: to the southwest of that river, and in the direction of the Floridas, the case was different. In most of the states situated to the southwest of the Hudson some great English proprietors had settled, who had imported with them aristocratic principles and the English law of descent. I have explained the reasons why it was impossible ever to establish a powerful aristocracy in America; these reasons existed with less force to the southwest of the Hudson. In the south, one man, aided by slaves, could cultivate a great extent of country: it was therefore common to see rich landed proprietors. But their influence was not altogether aristocratic as that term is understood in Europe, since they possessed no privileges; and the cultivation of their estates being carried on by slaves, they had no tenants depending on them, and consequently no patronage. Still, the great proprietors south of the Hudson constituted a superior class, having ideas and tastes of its own, and forming the centre of political action. This kind of aristocracy sympathized with the body of the people, whose passions and interests it easily embraced; but it was too weak and too short-lived to excite either love or hatred for itself. This was the class which headed the insurrection in the south, and furnished the best leaders of the American revolution.

At the period of which we are now speaking, society was shaken to its centre: the people, in whose name the struggle had taken place, conceived the desire of exercising the authority which it had acquired; its democratic tendencies were awakened; and having thrown off the yoke of the mother-country, it aspired to independence of every kind. The influence of individuals gradually ceased to be felt, and custom and law united together to produce the same result.

But the law of descent was the last step to equality. I am surprised that ancient and modern jurists have not attributed to this law a greater influence on human affairs. It is true that these laws belong to civil affairs: but they ought nevertheless to be placed at the head of all political institutions; for, while political laws are only the symbol of a nation's condition, they exercise an incredible influence upon its social state. They have, moreover, a sure and uniform manner of operating upon society, affecting, as it were, generations yet unborn.

Through their means man acquires a kind of preternatural power over the future lot of his fellow-creatures. When the legislator has once regulated the law of inheritance, he may rest from his labour. The machine once put in motion will go on for ages, and advance, as if self-guided, toward a given point. When framed in a particular manner, this law unites, draws together, and vests property and power in a few hands: its tendency is clearly aristocratic. On opposite principles its action is still more rapid; it divides, distributes, and disperses both property and power.

* * *

In the United States [the law of inheritance] has nearly completed its work of destruction, and there we can best study its results. The English laws concerning the transmission of property were abolished in almost all the states at the time of the revolution. The law of entail was so modified as not to interrupt the free circulation of property. The first having passed away, estates began to be parcelled out; and the change became more and more rapid with the progress of time. At this moment, after a lapse of little more than sixty years, the aspect of society is totally altered; the families of the great landed proprietors are almost all commingled with the general mass. In the state of New York, which formerly contained many of these, there are but two who still keep their heads above the stream; and they must shortly disappear. The sons of these opulent citizens have become merchants, lawyers, or physicians. Most of them have lapsed into obscurity. The last trace of hereditary ranks and distinctions is destroyed—the law of partition has reduced all to one level.

I do not mean that there is any deficiency of wealthy individuals in the United States; I know of no country, indeed, where the love of money has taken stronger hold on the affections of men, and where a profounder contempt is expressed for the theory of the permanent equality of property. But wealth circulates with inconceivable rapidity, and experience shows that it is rare to find two succeeding generations in the full enjoyment of it. . . .

It is not only the fortunes of men which are equal in America; even their acquirements partake in some degree of the same uniformity. I do not believe there is a country in the world where, in proportion to the population, there are so few uninstructed, and at the same time so few learned individuals. Primary instruction is within the reach of everybody; superior instruction is scarcely to be obtained by any. This is not surprising; it is in fact the necessary consequence of what we have advanced above. Almost all the Americans are in easy circumstances, and can therefore obtain the first elements of human knowledge.

In America there are comparatively few who are rich enough to live without a profession. Every profession requires an apprenticeship, which limits the time of instruction to the early years of life. At fifteen they enter upon their calling, and thus their education ends at the age when ours begins. Whatever is done afterward, is with a view to some special and lucrative object; a science is taken up as a matter of business, and the only branch of it which is attended to is such as admits of an immediate practical application.

In America most of the rich men were formerly poor: most of

those who now enjoy leisure were absorbed in business during their youth; the consequence of which is, that when they might have had a taste for study they had no time for it, and when the time is at their disposal they have no longer the inclination.

There is no class, then, in America in which the taste for intellectual pleasures is transmitted with hereditary fortune and leisure, and by which the labours of the intellect are held in honour. Accordingly there is an equal want of the desire and the power of application to these objects.

A middling standard is fixed in America for human knowledge. All approach as near to it as they can; some as they rise, others as they descend. Of course, an immense multitude of persons are to be found who entertain the same number of ideas on religion, history, science, political economy, legislation, and government. The gifts of intellect proceed directly from God, and man cannot prevent their unequal distribution. But in consequence of the state of things which we have here represented, it happens, that although the capacities of men are widely different, as the Creator has doubtless intended they should be, they are submitted to the same method of treatment.

In America the aristocratic element has always been feeble from its birth; and if at the present day it is not actually destroyed, it is at any rate so completely disabled that we can scarcely assign to it any degree of influence in the course of affairs.

The democratic principle, on the contrary, has gained so much strength by time, by events, and by legislation, as to have become not only predominant but all-powerful. There is no family or corporate authority, and it is rare to find even the influence of individual character enjoy any durability.

America, then, exhibits in her social state a most extraordinary phenomenon. Men are there seen on a greater equality in point of fortune and intellect, or in other words, more equal in their strength, than in any other country of the world, or, in any age of which history has preserved the remembrance.

Political Consequences of the Social Condition of the Anglo-Americans

The political consequences of such a social condition as this are easily deducible.

It is impossible to believe that equality will not eventually find its way into the political world as it does everywhere else. To conceive of men remaining for ever unequal upon one single point, yet equal on all others, is impossible; they must come in the end to be equal upon all.

Now I know of only two methods of establishing equality in the political world: every citizen must be put in possession of his rights, or rights must be granted to no one. For nations which have arrived at the same stage of social existence as the Anglo-Americans, it is therefore very difficult to discover a medium between the sovereignty of all and the absolute power of one man: and it would be vain to deny that the social condition which I have been describing is equally liable to each of these consequences.

There is, in fact, a manly and lawful passion for equality, which excites men to wish all to be powerful and honoured. This passion tends to elevate the humble to the rank of the great; but there exists also in the human heart a depraved taste for equality, which impels the weak to attempt to lower the powerful to their own level, and reduces men to prefer equality in slavery to inequality with freedom. Not that those nations whose social condition is democratic naturally despise liberty; on the contrary, they have an instinctive love of it. But liberty is not the chief and constant object of their desires; equality is their idol: they make rapid and sudden efforts to obtain liberty, and if they miss their aim, resign themselves to their disappointment; but nothing can satisfy them except equality, and rather than lose it they resolve to perish.

On the other hand, in a state where the citizens are nearly on an equality, it becomes difficult for them to preserve their independence against the aggressions of power. No one among them being strong enough to engage singly in the struggle with advantage, nothing but a general combination can protect their liberty: and such a union is not always to be found.

From the same social position, then, nations may derive one or the other of two great political results; these results are extremely different from each other, but they may both proceed from the same cause.

The Anglo-Americans are the first who, having been exposed to this formidable alternative, have been happy enough to escape the dominion of absolute power. They have been allowed by their circumstances, their origin, their intelligence, and especially by their moral feeling, to establish and maintain the sovereignty of the people.

*   *   *

Individualism Stronger at the Close of a Democratic Revolution than at Other Periods

. . . An aristocracy seldom yields without a protracted struggle, in the course of which implacable animosities are kindled between the different classes of society. These passions survive the victory, and traces of them may be observed in the midst of the democratic confusion which ensues.

Those members of the community who were at the top of the late gradations of rank cannot immediately forget their former greatness; they will long regard themselves as aliens in the midst of the newly composed society. They look upon all those whom this state of society has made their equals as oppressors, whose destiny can excite no sympathy; they have lost sight of their former equals, and feel no longer bound by a common interest to their fate: each of them, standing aloof, thinks that he is reduced to care for himself alone. Those, on the contrary, who were formerly at the foot of the social scale, and who have been brought up to the common level by a sudden revolution, cannot enjoy their newly acquired independence without secret uneasiness; and if they meet with some of their former superiors on the same footing as themselves, they stand aloof from them with an expression of triumph and of fear. . . .

The great advantage of the Americans is that they have arrived at a state of democracy without having to endure a democratic revolution; and that they are born equal, instead of becoming so.

*   *   *

Of Certain Peculiar and Accidental Causes Which Either Lead a People to Complete Centralization of Government, or Which Divert Them from It

. . . These observations explain why the supreme power is always stronger, and private individuals weaker, among a democratic people which has passed through a long and arduous struggle to reach a state of equality, than among a democratic community in which the citizens have been equal from the first. The example of the Americans completely demonstrates the fact. The inhabitants of the United States were never divided by any privileges; they have never known the mutual relation of master and inferior, and as they neither dread nor hate each other, they have never known the necessity of calling in the supreme power to manage

their affairs. The lot of the Americans is singular: they have derived from the aristocracy of England the notion of private rights
and the taste for local freedom; and they have been able to retain
both the one and the other, because they have had no aristocracy
to combat.

DANIEL J. BOORSTIN

The Genius of American Politics

*Daniel J. Boorstin is Professor of American History at the
University of Chicago and editor of the "Chicago History of
American Civilization." Among his books are* The Mysterious
Science of the Law *(1941);* The Lost World of Thomas Jef-
ferson *(1948);* The Genius of American Politics *(1953);* The
Americans *(1958 and 1965);* America and the Image of
Europe *(1960); and* The Image *(1962). In this selection
Boorstin maintains that the genius of American politics con-
sists in its imperviousness to ideology and systematic beliefs of
any kind.*

THE AMERICAN must go outside his country and hear the voice of
America to realize that his is one of the most spectacularly lop-
sided cultures in all history. The marvelous success and vitality of
our institutions is equaled by the amazing poverty and inarticulate-
ness of our theorizing about politics. No nation has ever believed
more firmly that its political life was based on a perfect theory.
And yet no nation has ever been less interested in political philosophy or produced less in the way of theory. If we can explain this
paradox, we shall have a key to much that is characteristic—and
much that is good—in our institutions.

In this chapter I shall attempt an explanation. I start from the
notion that the two sides of the paradox explain each other. The

very same facts which account for our belief that we actually possess a theory also explain why we have had little interest in political theories and have never bothered seriously to develop them.

For the belief that an explicit political theory is superfluous precisely because we already somehow possess a satisfactory equivalent, I propose the name "givenness." "Givenness" is the belief that values in America are in some way or other automatically defined: *given* by certain facts of geography or history peculiar to us. The notion, as I shall outline it in the present chapter, has three faces, which I shall describe in turn. First is the notion that we have received our values as a gift from the *past;* that the earliest settlers or Founding Fathers equipped our nation at its birth with a perfect and complete political theory, adequate to all our future needs.

The second is the notion that in America we receive values as a gift from the *present,* that our theory is always implicit in our institutions. This is the idea that the "American Way of Life" harbors an "American Way of Thought" which can do us for a political theory, even if we never make it explicit or never are in a position to confront ourselves with it. It is the notion that to Americans political theory never appears in its nakedness but always clothed in the peculiar American experience. We like to think that, from the shape of the living experience, we can guess what lies underneath and that such a guess is good enough—perhaps actually better than any naked theory. While according to the first axiom of "givenness" our values are the gift of our history, according to the second they are the gift of our landscape.

The third part of "givenness" is a belief which links these two axioms. It is a belief in the *continuity* or homogeneity of our history. It is the quality of our experience which makes us see our national past as an uninterrupted continuum of similar events, so that our past merges indistinguishably into our present. This sense of continuity is what makes it easy for us to accept the two first axioms at the same time: the idea of a preformed original theory given to us by the Founding Fathers, and the idea of an implicit theory always offered us by our present experience. Our feeling of continuity in our history makes it easy for us to see the Founding Fathers as our contemporaries. It induces us to draw heavily on the materials of our history, but always in a distinctly nonhistorical frame of mind.

I. Values Given by the Past: The Preformation Ideal

Now I shall begin by trying to explain what I have called the first axiom of "givenness": the idea that values are a gift from our past. Here we face our conscious attitude toward our past and toward our way of inheriting from it. This particular aspect of the "givenness" idea may be likened to the obsolete biological notion of "preformation." That is the idea that all parts of an organism pre-exist in perfect miniature in the seed. Biologists used to believe that if you could look at the seed of an apple under a strong enough microscope you would see in it a minute apple tree. Similarly, we seem still to believe that if we could understand the ideas of the earliest settlers—the Pilgrim Fathers or Founding Fathers—we would find in them no mere seventeenth- or eighteenth-century philosophy of government but the perfect embryo of the theory by which we now live. We believe, then, that the mature political ideals of the nation existed clearly conceived in the minds of our patriarchs. The notion is essentially static. It assumes that the values and theory of the nation were given once and for all in the very beginning.

What circumstances of American history have made such a view possible? The first is the obvious fact that, unlike western European countries, where the coming of the first white man is shrouded in prehistoric mist, civilization in the United States stems from people who came to the American continent at a definite period in recent history. For American political thought this fact has had the greatest significance. We have not found it necessary to invent an Aeneas, for we have had our William Bradford and John Winthrop, or, looking to a later period, our Benjamin Franklin and James Madison. We have needed no Virgil to make a myth of the first settlement of our land or the first founding of the Republic; the crude facts of history have been good enough.

The facts of our history have thus made it easy for us to assume that our national life, as distinguished from that of the European peoples who trace their identity to a remote era, has had a clear purpose. Life in America—appropriately called "The American Experiment"—has again and again been described as the test or the proof of values supposed to have been clearly in the minds of the Founders. While, as we shall see, the temper of much of our thought has been antihistorical, it is nevertheless true that we have leaned heavily on history to clarify our image of ourselves. Perhaps never before, except conceivably in the modern state of

Israel, has a nation so firmly believed that it was founded on a full-blown theory and hence that it might understand itself by re-capturing a particular period in its past. . . .

Our determination to believe in a single logically complete theory as our heritage from the earliest settlers has thus actually kept us from grasping the *facts* of the early life of our nation. Strenuous efforts have been made to homogenize all the fathers of our country. A great deal of the popular misunderstanding of the New England Puritans, for example, can be traced to this desire. Tradition teaches us to treat the history of our nation from 1620 to 1789 as a series of labor pains, varying only in intensity. The Puritans, we are taught, came here for religious and political liberty; and the American Revolutionaries are supposed to have shown a pilgrim-like fervor and clarity of purpose.

If we compare our point of view with that of the historically conscious peoples of Europe, we shall begin to see some of its implications. The Europeans have, of course, had their interludes of nostalgia for some mythical heroic age, some Wagnerian Göt-terdämmerung. Mussolini sought to reincarnate the Roman Em-pire, Hitler to revive some prehistoric "Aryan" community. But such efforts in Europe have been spasmodic. Europeans have not with any continuity attributed to their nameless "earliest settlers" the mature ideals of their national life. In contrast, we have been consistently primitivistic. The brevity of our history has made this way of thinking easy. Yet that is not the whole story. We find it peculiarly congenial to claim possession of a perfect set of politi-cal ideas, especially when they have magical elusiveness and flexi-bility. Their mere existence seems to relieve us of an unwelcome task.

Our firm belief in a perfectly preformed theory helps us under-stand many things about ourselves. In particular, it helps us see how it has been that, while we in the United States have been unfertile in political theories, we have at the same time possessed an over-weening sense of orthodoxy. The poverty of later theorizing has encouraged appeal to what we like to believe went before. In building an orthodoxy from sparse materials, of necessity we have left the penumbra of heresy vague. The inarticulate character of American political theory has thus actually facilitated heresy-hunts and tended to make them indiscriminate. The heresy-hunts which come at periods of national fear—the Alien and Sedition Acts of the age of the French Revolution, the Palmer raids of the age of the Russian Revolution, and similar activities of more recent times—are directed not so much against acts of espionage as against acts of irreverence toward that orthodox American creed, believed to have been born with the nation itself. . . .

The fact that we have had a written constitution, and even our special way of interpreting it, has contributed to the "preformation" notion. Changes in our policy or our institutions are read back into the ideas, and sometimes into the very words, of the Founding Fathers. Everybody knows that this had made of our federal Constitution an "unwritten" document. What is more significant is the way in which we have justified the adaptation of the document to current needs: by attributing clarity, comprehensiveness, and a kind of mystical foresight to the social theory of the founders. In Great Britain, where there is an "unwritten" constitution in a very different sense, constitutional theory has taken for granted the *gradual* formulation of a theory of society. No sensible Briton would say that his history is the unfolding of the truths implicit in Magna Charta and the Bill of Rights. Such documents are seen as only single steps in a continuing process of definition. . . .

If we turn from our constitution to our political parties, we observe the same point of view. The authority of a particular past generation implies the impotence of later generations to reconstruct the theoretical bases of our national life. Today it is still taken for granted that the proper arena of controversy was marked off once and for all in the late eighteenth century: we are either Jeffersonians or Hamiltonians.

In no other country has the hagiography of politics been more important. The lives of our national saints have remained vivid and contemporary for us. In no other country—except perhaps in Soviet Russia, where people are called Marxists, Leninists, or Trotskyites—do statesmen so intimately embrace the image of early national heroes. Would an Englishman call himself a Walpolean or a Pittite? Yet in the United States the very names of our political parties—Republican and Democratic—are borrowed from the early age of our national life. This remarkable persistence of early labels offers the sharpest contrast to what we see in continental western Europe. There new parties—and new party labels —come and go with the seasons, and most of the parties, with double- or triple-barreled names, draw on the novel vocabulary of the nineteenth and twentieth centuries. It is a commonplace that no fundamental theoretical difference separates our American political parties. What need has either party for an explicit political theory when both must be spokesmen of the *original* American doctrine on which the nation was founded?

*   *   *

The mystic rigidity of our "preformation" theory has been consistent with great flexibility in dealing with practical problems. Confident that the wisdom of the Founding Fathers somehow made provision for all future emergencies, we have not felt bound to limit our experiments to those which we could justify with theories in advance. In the last century or so, whenever the citizens of continental western Europe have found themselves in desperate circumstances, they have had to choose among political parties, each of which was committed to a particular theoretical foundation for its whole program—"monarchist," "liberal," "catholic," "socialist," "fascist," or "communist." This has not been the case in the United States. Not even during the Civil War: historians still argue over what, if any, political theory Lincoln represented. In the crisis which followed the great depression, when Franklin D. Roosevelt announced his program for saving the American economy, he did not promise to implement a theory. Rather, he declared frankly that he would try one thing after another and would keep trying until a cure was found. "The country demands bold, persistent experimentation. It is common sense to take a method and try it: if it fails, admit it frankly and try another." Neither he nor his listeners doubted that whatever solution, within the limits of common-law liberties, might prove successful would also prove to have been within the prevision of the Founding Fathers. The people balked only when a proposal—like the Court-packing plan—seemed to imperil the independence of the judiciary, an ancient principle of the common law. . . .

Our mystic belief in the "preformed" national theory has . . . restrained theoretical vagaries without preventing particular experiments. Without having ever intended it, we have thus stumbled on an evolutionary approach to institutions. Yet at the same time we have taken up a kind of social Freudianism; for the "preformation" concept of values implies belief that the childhood years of a nation's history are crucial for the formation of its character. More than that, we have given the national past a pe-

culiarly normative significance. Small wonder that we should seem
complacent, if we judge ourselves by whether we are true to our
own character. Our American past and the theories of politics
which it is thought to imply, have become the yardstick against
which national life is measured. This is the deeper meaning of
the criterion of "Americanism" which is so familiar in the United
States and sounds so strange to European ears.

II. Values Given by the Landscape:
The Land of the Free

. . . The second axiom is similar, in that it, too, is an excuse or a
reason for not philosophizing. It is the notion that a scheme of
values is given, not by traditions, theories, books, and institutions,
but by present experience. It is the notion that our theory of life
is embodied in our way of life and need not be separated from it,
that our values are given by our condition. If this second part of
the idea of "givenness" seems, in strict logic, contradictory to the
first, from the point of view of the individual believer it is actually
complementary. For, while the first axiom is ideal and static in
its emphasis, the second is practical and dynamic. "Preformation"
means that the theory of community was given, once and for all,
in the beginning; the second sense of "givenness" means that
the theory of community is perpetually being given and ever
anew.

Taken together with the idea of preformation, this second "givenness" makes an amazingly comprehensive set of attitudes. The
American is thus prepared to find in *all* experience—in his history
and his geography, in his past and his present—proof for his conviction that he is equipped with a hierarchy of values, a political
theory. Both axioms together encourage us to think that we need
not invent a political theory because we already possess one. The
idea of "givenness" as a whole is, then, both as idealistic as a
prophet's vision and as hardheaded as common sense.

This second face of "givenness" is at once much simpler and
much more vague than the concept of preformation. It is simply
the notion that values are implicit in the American experience.
The idea that the American landscape is a giver of values is, of
course, old and familiar. It has long been believed that in America the community values would not have to be sought through
books, traditions, the messianic vision of prophets, or the specula-
tive schemes of philosophers but would somehow be the gift of the
continent itself.

We Americans have always been much impressed by the simple fact that we are children of a Brave New World. Even from the earliest settlements, but especially since the formative era of the late eighteenth and early nineteenth centuries, we have looked upon ourselves as the lucky beneficiaries of an especially happy environment. In the pamphlets which Puritans wrote in the seventeenth century to attract their brethren to New England, we read fantastic tales of the abundance of crops and game, the magic of the air and water; how life on the new continent cured consumption, gout, and all sorts of fevers; how the old became young, the young became vigorous, and barren women suddenly bore children. In the very same pamphlet we can read how the wilderness would toughen the effete and how the wealth of this unexploited paradise would enrich the impoverished. . . .

Our belief in the mystical power of our land has in this roundabout way nourished an empirical point of view; and a naturalistic approach to values has thus, in the United States, been bound up with patriotism itself. What the Europeans have seen as the gift of the past, Americans have seen as the gift of the present. What the European thinks he must learn from books, museums, and churches, from his culture and its monuments, the American thinks he can get from contemporary life, from seizing peculiarly American opportunities.

*　　*　　*

The very commonness of American values has seemed their proof: they have come directly from the hand of God and from the soil of the continent. This attitude helps explain why the martyr (at least the *secular* martyr) has not been attractive to us. In the accurate words of our popular song, "The Best Things in Life Are Free." Men in America have had to struggle against nature, against wild Indians, high mountains, arid deserts, against space itself. But these struggles have seemed required to make the continent livable or comfortable, not to make our society good. In Europe, on the other hand, the liberal could not make the plant of liberty grow without first cutting out the weeds of tyranny; and he took that for his task. But the American has preened himself on his good sense in making *his* home where liberty is the natural growth. Voltaire declared, "Where liberty is not, there is my home." This was a fitting and thoroughly un-American reply to Franklin's "Where liberty dwells, there is my country."

The character of our national heroes bears witness to our belief in "givenness," our preference for the man who seizes his God-given opportunities over him who pursues a great private vision. Perhaps never before has there been such a thorough identification of normality and virtue. A "red-blooded" American must be a virtuous American; and nearly all our national heroes have been red-blooded, outdoor types who might have made the varsity team. Our ideal is at the opposite pole from that of a German Super-man or an irredentist agitator in his garret. We admire not the monstrous but the normal, not the herald of a new age but the embodiment of his own. In the language of John Dewey, he is the well-adjusted man; in the language of Arthur Miller's Salesman, Willy Loman, he is the man who is not merely liked but *well-liked*. Our national heroes have not been erratic geniuses like Michelangelo or Cromwell or Napoleon but rather men like Wash-ington and Jackson and Lincoln, who possessed the commonplace virtues to an extraordinary degree.

III. The Continuity of American History

The third part of the idea of "givenness," as I have said, is actually a kind of link between the two axioms which I have al-ready described: the notion that we have an ideal given in a par-ticular period in the past (what I have called the idea of "pre-formation") and the idea that the theory of American life is always being given anew in the present, that values are implicit in the American experience. The third aspect to which I now turn helps us understand how we can at once appeal to the past and yet be fervently unhistorical in our approach to it.

By this I mean the remarkable continuity or homogeneity of American history. To grasp it, we must at the outset discard a European cliché about us, namely, that ours is a land without con-tinuity or tradition, while in Europe man feels close to his an-cestors. The truth of the matter is that anyone who goes to Europe nowadays cannot fail to be impressed with the amazing, the unique, continuity of American history and, in sharp con-trast, the *dis*continuity of European history.

This is true in several senses. In the first place, there is the ob-vious fact that the recent history of Europe has seen violent oscil-lations of regime. Each new regime has taken on itself a task of historical amnesia: the fascists trying to deny their democratic past, the democrats trying to deny their fascist past, etc. But there is a subtler way in which the landscape and monuments which surround the European tend to impress on him the various possibilities of life in his place, while what the American sees confirms his sense of "givenness," his belief in the normality, if not the inevitability, of the particular institutions which he has evolved. "For the American tourist," Aldous Huxley has shrewdly observed, "the greatest charm of foreign travel is the very high ratio of European history to European geography. Conversely, for the European, who has come to feel the oppressive weight of a doubtless splendid, but often fatal past, the greatest charm of travel in the New World is the high ratio of its geography to its history.". . .

In Europe one need not be an archeologist or a philosopher to see that over the centuries many different kinds of life are possible in the same place and for the same people. Who can decide which, if any of these, is "normal" for Italy? It is hardly surprising, then, that the people of Europe have not found it easy to believe that their values are given by their landscape. They look to ideology to help them choose among alternatives.

In the United States, of course, we see no Colosseum, no Capella Palatina, no ancient roads. The effect of this simple fact on our aesthetic sense, though much talked of, is probably less significant than on our sense of history and our approach to values. We see very few monuments to the uncertainties, the motley possibilities, of history or, for that matter, to the rise and fall of grand theories of society. Our main public buildings were erected for much the same purpose for which they are now being used. The Congress of the United States is still housed in the first building expressly constructed for that purpose. . . .

The impression which the American has as he looks about him is one of the inevitability of the particular institutions, the particular kind of society in which he lives. The kind of acceptance of institutions as proper to their time and place which tyrants have labored in vain to produce has in the United States been the result of the accidents of history. The limitations of our history have perhaps confined our philosophical imagination; but they have at the same time confirmed our sense of the continuity of our past and made the definitions of philosophers seem less urgent. We Americans are reared with a feeling for the unity of our history and an unprecedented belief in the normality of our kind of life to our place on earth.

We have just been observing that our history has had a continuity: that is, that the same political institutions have persisted throughout our whole national career and therefore have acquired a certain appearance of normality and inevitableness. No less important is the converse of this fact, namely, that our history has *not* been *dis*continuous, has not been punctuated by the kind of internal struggles which have marked the history of most of the countries of western Europe, and which have fed their awareness that society is shaped by men. . . .The important fact is what De Tocqueville observed a century ago, namely, that America somehow has reaped the fruits of the long democratic revolution in Europe "without having had the revolution itself." This was but another way of saying that the prize for which Europeans would have to shed blood would seem the free native birthright of Americans.

During these last one hundred and seventy-five years the history of the United States has thus had a unity and coherence unknown in Europe. Many factors—our geographical isolation, our special opportunities for expansion and exploitation within our own borders, and our remoteness from Europe—have, of course, contributed. Even our American Civil War, which shook us deeply and was one of the bloodiest wars anywhere in the century, can be understood with scant reference to the ideologies then sweeping Europe: to the intellectual background of 1848, of the Risorgimento, of the Paris Commune. It was not properly a counterpart of European struggles of the period, nor really an exception to the domestic continuity of our history.

But, whatever the causes, the winds of dogma and the gusts of revolution which during the last century and a half have blown violently over western Europe, making France, Italy, Germany, and now perhaps even England testing grounds for panaceas, have not ruffled our intellectual climate. The United States, with a kind of obstinate provincialism, has enjoyed relatively calm weather. While European politics became a kaleidoscope, political life in the United States has seemed to remain a window through which we can look at the life envisaged by our patriarchs. The hills and valleys of European history in the nineteenth century have had no real counterpart in the history of the United States. Because our road has been relatively smooth, we have easily believed that we have trod no historical road at all. We seem the direct beneficiaries of our climate, our soil, and our mineral wealth.

LOUIS HARTZ
The Concept of a Liberal Society

*Louis Hartz, Professor of Government at Harvard University,
is the author of* Economic Policy and Democratic Thought
(1948); The Liberal Tradition in America *(1955), which was
awarded the Woodrow Wilson Prize of the American Political
Science Association; and* The Founding of New Societies
*(1964). In this selection from his second book Hartz argues
that there have not been any fundamental divisions in ideology
in American politics ultimately because of two factors: the
absence of the legacies of revolution and reaction which feudalism left in Europe; and the presence of an original liberal
principle brought by the segment of English society that settled
here, which grew without substantial obstruction from any contrary political principle.*

THE ANALYSIS . . . IS BASED on what might be called the storybook
truth about American history: that America was settled by men
who fled from the feudal and clerical oppressions of the Old World.
If there is anything in this view, as old as the national folklore
itself, then the outstanding thing about the American community
in Western history ought to be the nonexistence of those oppressions, or since the reaction against them was in the broadest sense
liberal, that the American community is a liberal community. We
are confronted, as it were, with a kind of inverted Trotskyite law
of combined development, America skipping the feudal stage of
history as Russia presumably skipped the liberal stage. . . .
   One of the central characteristics of a nonfeudal society is that
it lacks a genuine revolutionary tradition, the tradition which in
Europe has been linked with the Puritan and French revolutions:

that it is "born free," as Tocqueville said. And this being the case, it lacks also a tradition of reaction: lacking Robespierre it lacks Maistre, lacking Sydney it lacks Charles II. Its liberalism is what Santayana called, referring to American democracy, a "natural" phenomenon. But the matter is curiously broader than this, for a society which begins with Locke, and thus transforms him, stays with Locke, by virtue of an absolute and irrational attachment it develops for him, and becomes as indifferent to the challenge of socialism in the later era as it was unfamiliar with the heritage of feudalism in the earlier one. It has within it, as it were, a kind of self-completing mechanism, which insures the universality of the liberal idea. Here, we shall see, is one of the places where Marx went wrong in his historical analysis, attributing as he did the emergence of the socialist ideology to the objective movement of economic forces. Actually socialism is largely an ideological phe-nomenon, arising out of the principles of class and the revolu-tionary liberal revolt against them which the old European order inspired. It is not accidental that America which has uniquely lacked a feudal tradition has uniquely lacked also a socialist tra-dition. The hidden origin of socialist thought everywhere in the West is to be found in the feudal ethos. The *ancien régime* inspires Rousseau; both inspire Marx. . . .

Now if the *ancien régime* is not present to begin with, one thing follows automatically: it does not return in a blaze of glory. It does not flower in the nineteenth century in a Disraeli or a Bal-lanche, however different from each other these men may be. I do not mean to imply that no trace of the feudal urge, no shadow whatsoever of Sir Walter Scott, has been found on the hills and plains of the New World. One can get into a lot of useless argu-ment if he affirms the liberalness of a liberal society in absolute mathematical fashion. The top strata of the American community, from the time of Peggy Hutchinson to the time of Margaret Ken-nedy, have yearned for the aristocratic ethos. But instead of ex-emplifying the typical Western situation, these yearnings represent an inversion of it. America has presented the world with the pe-culiar phenomenon, not of a frustrated middle class, but of a "frustrated aristocracy"—of men, Aristotelian-like, trying to break out of the egalitarian confines of middle class life but suffering guilt and failure in the process. The South before the Civil War is the case par excellence of this, though New England of course exemplifies it also. Driven away from Jefferson by abolitionism, the Fitzhughs of the ante-bellum era actually dared to ape the doctrinal patterns of the Western reaction, of Disraeli and Bonald. But when Jefferson is traditional, European traditionalism is a curious thing indeed. The Southerners were thrown into fantastic contradictions by their iconoclastic conservatism, by what I have called the "Reactionary Enlightenment," and after the Civil War for good historical reasons they fell quickly into oblivion. The South, as John Crowe Ransom has said, has been the part of America closest to Old World Europe, but it has never really been Europe. It has been an alien child in a liberal family, tortured and confused, driven to a fantasy life which, instead of disproving the power of Locke in America, portrays more poignantly than anything else the tyranny he has had.

But is not the problem of Fitzhugh at once the problem of De Leon? Here we have one of the great and neglected relationships in American history: the common fecklessness of the Southern "feudalists" and the modern socialists. It is not accidental, but something rooted in the logic of all of Western history, that they should fail alike to leave a dent in the American liberal intelligence. For if the concept of class was meaningless in its Disraelian form, and if American liberalism had never acquired it in its bourgeois form, why should it be any more meaningful in its Marxian form? This secret process of ideological transmission is not, however, the only thing involved. Socialism arises not only to fight capitalism but remnants of feudalism itself, so that the failure of the Southern Filmerians, in addition to setting the pattern for the failure of the later Marxists, robbed them in the process of a normal ground for growth. Could De Leon take over the liberal goal of extended suffrage as Lasalle did in Germany or the crusade against the House of Lords as the Labor Party did in England? Marx himself noted the absence of an American feudalism, but since he misinterpreted the complex origins of European socialism in the European *ancien régime,* he did not grasp the significance of it.

Surely, then, it is a remarkable force: this fixed, dogmatic liberalism of a liberal way of life. It is the secret root from which have sprung many of the most puzzling of American cultural phenomena. Take the unusual power of the Supreme Court and the cult of constitution worship on which it rests. Federal factors apart, judicial review as it has worked in America would be inconceivable without the national acceptance of the Lockian creed, ultimately enshrined in the Constitution, since the removal of high policy to the realm of adjudication implies a prior recognition of the principles to be legally interpreted. At the very moment that Senator Benton was hailing the rise of America's constitutional fetishism, in France Royer Collard and the Doctrinaires were desperately trying to build precisely the same atmosphere around the Restoration Charter of 1814, but being a patchwork of Maistre and Rousseau, that constitutional document exploded in their faces in the July Revolution. . . . If in England a marvelous organic cohesion has held together the feudal, liberal, and socialist ideas, it would still be unthinkable there that the largest issues of public policy should be put before nine Talmudic judges examining a single text. But this is merely another way of saying that law has flourished on the corpse of philosophy in America, for the settlement of the ultimate moral question is the end of speculation upon it. Pragmatism, interestingly enough America's great contribution to the philosophic tradition, does not alter this, since it feeds itself on the Lockian settlement. It is only when you take your ethics for granted that all problems emerge as problems of technique. Not that this is a bar in America to institutional innovations of highly non-Lockian kind. Indeed, as the New Deal shows, when you simply "solve problems" on the basis of a submerged and absolute liberal faith, you can depart from Locke with a kind of inventive freedom that European Liberal reformers and even European socialists, dominated by ideological systems, cannot duplicate. But the main point remains: if Fitzhugh and De Leon were crucified by the American general will, John Marshall and John Dewey flourished in consequence of their crucifixion. The moral unanimity of a liberal society reaches out in many directions.

At bottom it is riddled with paradox. Here is a Lockian doctrine which in the West as a whole is the symbol of rationalism, yet in America the devotion to it has been so irrational that it has not even been recognized for what it is: liberalism. There has never been a "liberal movement" or a real "liberal party" in America: we have only had the American Way of Life, a nationalist articulation of Locke which usually does not know that Locke himself is involved; and we did not even get that until after the Civil War when the Whigs of the nation, deserting the Hamiltonian tradition, saw the capital that could be made out of it. This is why even critics who have noticed America's moral unity have usually missed its substance. Ironically, "liberalism" is a stranger in the land of its greatest realization and fulfillment. But this is not all. Here is a doctrine which everywhere in the West has been a glorious symbol of individual liberty, yet in America its compulsive power has been so great that it has posed a threat to liberty itself. Actually Locke has a hidden conformitarian germ to begin with, since natural law tells equal people equal things, but when this germ is fed by the explosive power of modern nationalism, it mushrooms into something pretty remarkable. One can reasonably wonder about the liberty one finds in Burke.

I believe that this is the basic ethical problem of a liberal society: not the danger of the majority which has been its conscious fear, but the danger of unanimity, which has slumbered unconsciously behind it: the "tyranny of opinion" that Tocqueville saw unfolding as even the pathetic social distinctions of the Federalist era collapsed before his eyes. But in recent times this manifestation of irrational Lockianism, or of "Americanism," to use a favorite term of the American Legion, one of the best expounders of the national spirit that Whiggery discovered after the Civil War, has neither slumbered nor been unconscious. It has been very much awake in a red scare hysteria which no other nation in the West has really been able to understand. And this suggests a very significant principle: that when a liberal community faces military and ideological pressure from without it transforms eccentricity into sin, and the irritating figure of the bourgeois gossip flowers into the frightening figure of an A. Mitchell Palmer or a Senator [Joseph R.] McCarthy. Do we not find here, hidden away at the base of the American mind, one of the reasons why its legalism has been so imperfect a barrier against the violent moods of its mass Lockianism? If the latter is nourished by the former, how can we expect it to be strong? We say of the Supreme Court that it is courageous when it challenges Jefferson, but since in a liberal society the individualism of Hamilton is also a secret part of the Jeffersonian psyche, we make too much of this. The real test of the Court is when it faces the excitement both of Jefferson and Hamilton, when the Talmudic text is itself at stake, when the general will on which it feeds rises to the surface in anger. And here, brave as the Court has been at moments, its record has been no more heroic than the logic of the situation would suggest.

The decisive domestic issue of our time may well lie in the counter resources a liberal society can muster against this deep and unwritten tyrannical compulsion it contains. They exist. Given the individualist nature of the Lockian doctrine, there is always a

logical impulse within it to transcend the very conformitarian
spirit it breeds in a Lockian society: witness the spirit of Holmes
and Hand. . . .

But the most powerful force working to shatter the American
absolutism is, paradoxically enough, the very international involvement which intensifies it. This involvement is complex in its implications. If in the context of the Russian Revolution it elicits a domestic redscare, in the context of diplomacy it elicits an impulse
to impose Locke everywhere. The way in which "Americanism"
brings McCarthy together with Wilson is of great significance and
it is, needless to say, another one of Progressivism's neglected roots
in the Rousseauan tide it often seeks to stem. Thus to say that
world politics shatters "Americanism" at the moment it intensifies
it is to say a lot: it is to say that the basic horizons of the nation
both at home and abroad are drastically widened by it. But has
this not been the obvious experience of the recent past? Along with
the fetish that has been made of Locke at peace conferences and at
Congressional investigations has not Locke suffered a relativistic
beating at the same time? You can turn the issue of Wilsonianism
upside down: when has the nation appreciated more keenly the
limits of its own cultural pattern as applied to the rest of the
world? You can turn the issue of McCarthyism upside down:
when has the meaning of civil liberties been more ardently understood than now? A dialectic process is at work, evil eliciting
the challenge of a conscious good, so that in difficult moments
progress is made. The outcome of the battle between intensified
"Americanism" and new enlightenment is still an open question.

Historically the issue here is one for which we have little prec-
edent. It raises the question of whether a nation can compensate
for the uniformity of its domestic life by contact with alien cultures outside it. It asks whether American liberalism can acquire
through external experience that sense of relativity, that spark of
philosophy which European liberalism acquired through an internal experience of social diversity and social conflict. But if the
final problem posed by the American liberal community is bizarre,
this is merely a continuation of its historic record. That community
has always been a place where the common issues of the West
have taken strange and singular shape. . . .

So far I have spoken of natural liberalism as a psychological
whole, embracing the nation and inspiring unanimous decisions.

We must not assume, however, that this is to obscure or to minimize the nature of the internal conflicts which have characterized
American political life. . . . What we learn from the concept of a
liberal society, lacking feudalism and therefore socialism and
governed by an irrational Lockianism, is that the domestic struggles of such a society have all been projected with the setting of
Western liberal alignments. . . .

We can thus say of the right in America that it exemplifies
the tradition of big propertied liberalism in Europe. . . . It is the
tradition which embraces loosely the English Presbyterian and the
English Whig, the French Girondin and the French Liberal: a tradition which hates the *ancien régime* up to a certain point, loves
capitalism, and fears democracy. Occasionally, as a matter of
fact, American Hamiltonianism has been called by the English
term "Whiggery," though no effort has been made to pursue the
comparative analysis which this label suggests. Similarly the
European "petit-bourgeois" tradition is the starting point for an
understanding of the American left. Here, to be sure, there are
critical problems of identification, since one of the main things
America did was to expand and transform the European "petit-
bourgeois" by absorbing both the peasantry and the proletariat
into the structure of his personality. . . .

One of the reasons these European liberal correlations have
gone neglected is quite obvious once you try to make them.
America represents the liberal mechanism of Europe functioning
without the European social antagonisms, but the truth is, it is only
through these antagonisms that we recognize the mechanism. We
know the European liberal, as it were, by the enemies he has
made: take them away in American fashion and he does not seem
like the same man at all. This is true even of the Whig who
prior to 1840 poses the easiest problem in this respect. Remove
Wellington from Macaulay, and you have in essence Alexander
Hamilton, but the link between the latter two is not at first easy
to see. After 1840, when the American Whig gives up his Hamiltonian elitism and discovers the Horatio Alger ethos of a liberal
society, discovers "Americanism," the task of identification is
even harder. For while it is true that the liberals of England
and France ultimately accepted political democracy, Algerism
and "Americanism" were social ideologies they could hardly
exploit. So that the continuing problem of a missing Toryism,
which is enough to separate the American Republicans from the

reactionary liberals of Victorian England and the Neo-Girondins
of the Third Republic, is complicated further by the unique
ideological shape that the Whig tradition is destined to take in a
liberal society.

The American democrat, that "petit-bourgeois" hybrid of the
American world, raises even more intricate questions. To take
away the Social Republic from the French Montagnards changes
their appearance just about as much as taking away the feudal
right from the English Whigs. But the American democrat, alas,
deviated sharply from the Montagnards to begin with, since in
addition to being "petit-bourgeois" in their sense he was a
liberal peasant and a liberal proletarian as well: indeed the whole
of the nation apart from the Whig, a condition hardly vouchsafed
to the Montagnards. And yet even in the face of such tremendous
variations, comparative analysis can continue. We have to tear
the giant figure of Jackson apart, sorting out not only the "petit-
bourgeois" element of the man but those rural and urban elements
which the American liberal community has transformed. Ultimately,
as with the Whigs, for all of the magical chemistry of American
liberal society, we are dealing with social materials common to
the Western world.

That society has been a triumph for the liberal idea, but we
must not assume that this ideological victory was not helped
forward by the magnificent material setting it found in the New
World. The agrarian and proletarian strands of the American democratic personality, which in some sense typify the whole of
American uniqueness, reveal a remarkable collusion between
Locke and the New World. Had it been merely the liberal spirit
alone which inspired the American farmer to become capital-
istically oriented, to repudiate save for a few early remnants the
village organization of Europe, to produce for a market and
even to enter capitalist occupations on the side such as logging
and railroad building, then the difficulties he encountered would
have been greater than they were. But where land was abundant
and the voyage to the New World itself a claim to independence,
the spirit which repudiated peasantry and tenantry flourished
with remarkable ease. Similarly, had it merely been an aspect of
irrational Lockianism which inspired the American worker to
think in terms of the capitalist setup, the task would have been
harder than it was.

But social fluidity was peculiarly fortified by the riches of a rich land, so that there was no small amount of meaning to Lincoln's claim in 1861 that the American laborer, instead of "being fixed to that condition for life," works for "a while," then "saves," then "hires another beginner" as he himself becomes an entrepreneur. And even when factory industrialism gained sway after the Civil War, and the old artisan and cottage-and-mill mentality was definitely gone, it was still a Lockian idea fortified by material resources which inspired the triumph of the job mentality of Gompers rather than the class mentality of the European worker. The "petit-bourgeois" giant of America, though ultimately a triumph for the liberal idea, could hardly have chosen a better material setting in which to flourish.

But a liberal society does not merely produce old Whig and new democrat, does not merely cast a strange set of lights and shadows on them. More crucially it shapes the outcome of the struggle in which they engage. . . .

Firstly America, by making its "petit-bourgeois" hybrid the mass of the nation, makes him unconquerable, save in two instances: when he is disorganized, as prior to Jefferson and Jackson, or when he is enchanted with the dream of becoming a Whig himself, as prior to the crash of 1929. Which is merely another way of saying the the historic Whig technique of *divide et impera* which comes out perhaps most vividly at the time of the First Reform Act and the July Revolution—of playing the mass against the *ancien régime,* the *ancien régime* against the mass, and the mass against itself—cannot work in a society where the mass embraces everything but Whiggery. This is what the Hamiltonian Federalists, who actually tried to pursue this course in America, ultimately had to learn. And this is also why, when they learned it, even their existing resemblance to European Whiggery disappeared and they became distinctively American operators. What they learned was the Alger mechanism of enchanting the American democrat and the "Americanistic" mechanism of terrifying him, which was the bounty they were destined to receive for the European strategies of which they were deprived. For the defeat of Hamilton, so long as the economy boomed, they were bound to get the victory of McKinley. One might call this the great law of Whig compensation inherent in American politics. The record of its functioning takes up a large part of American history.

So one cannot say of the liberal society analysis that by concentrating on national unities it rules out the meaning of domestic conflict. Actually it discovers that meaning, which is obscured by the very Progressive analysis that presumably concentrates on conflict. You do not get closer to the significance of an earthquake by ignoring the terrain on which it takes place. On the contrary, that is one of the best ways of making sure that you will miss its significance. The argument over whether we should "stress" solidarity or conflict in American politics misleads us by advancing a false set of alternatives.

JOHN HIGHAM

The Cult of Consensus

John Higham, Professor of History at the University of Michigan, has written Strangers in the Land *(1955) and* History *(1965). He is also the author of a number of articles dealing with past, current, and emergent trends in American historiography. The following selection from one of these articles contrasts the traditional Progressive interpretation of American political development, which emphasized conflict, with a tendency, of the 1950's, to view American political development in Neo-Tocquevillean and dominantly consensual terms.*

IN RETROSPECT, it is becoming apparent that the decade of the 1940's marked a fundamental change of direction in the exploration of the American past. At the time nothing very unusual seemed to be happening in the minds of American historians, in spite of the clamor in the world around them. The usual outpouring of conventional monographs continued. Our endless fascination with the pageant of the Civil War produced a new but not a very different crop of narratives. There was, to be sure, a rising volume of criticism of the giants who had dominated American historical scholarship

Reprinted from John Higham, "The Cult of the 'American Consensus': Homogenizing our History," *Commentary*, XXVII (February, 1959), 93-97, 99-100, by permission. Copyright © 1959 by the American Jewish Committee.

in the period between the wars: Frederick Jackson Turner, Charles A. Beard, and Vernon L. Parrington. But the image they had fixed on the screen of the American past had only begun to dissolve. . . .

In the last few years, however, the critical attacks of the 40's have matured into a full-scale reappraisal of the main themes in American history. The great trio of yesteryear have gone into eclipse. Their vision of an America in which democracy, vaguely associated with the West, battled against entrenched economic privilege no longer seems basic enough to define the shape of our national development. On the whole, the distinctive interpretations of Turner, Beard, and Parrington no longer appear persuasive enough to evoke really lively controversy. They linger on, flattened and desiccated, in the pages of many a textbook, where they may occasionally inflame the Daughters of the American Revolution, the *Daily News,* and others who specialize in discovering the menace of dead issues. Meanwhile, our living historical awareness has moved so far from the interests of Turner, Beard, and Parrington that interpretive historians now feel less need to criticize or defend them than to supersede them. . . .

An earlier generation of historians, inspired by Turner, Beard, and Parrington and nurtured in a restless atmosphere of reform, had painted America in the bold hues of conflict. Sometimes their interpretations pitted class against class, sometimes section against section; and increasingly they aligned both sections and classes behind the banners of clashing ideologies. It was East vs. West, with the South gravitating from one to the other; farmers vs. businessmen, with urban workers in the pivotal position; city vs. country; property rights vs. human rights; Hamiltonianism vs. Jeffersonianism. These lines of cleavage were charted continuously from the Colonial period to the present. They gave a sense of depth to the social struggles which historians in the early 20th century observed all around them.

The divisions between periods loomed as large as those between groups. Among scholars attuned to conflict, American history appeared jagged and discontinuous. Historians like Beard had an eye for the convulsive moments in history, and they dramatized vividly the turning points when one side or the other seemed to seize control. To them, America had had several revolutions, usually triumphant over formidable resistance, and always big with unfulfilled promise. They saw the revolution of 1776 not

simply as a war for independence but as a drastic redistribution
of power within the Colonies. They called the Civil War the
"Second American Revolution," and in between they acclaimed
the "Revolution of 1800," when Jefferson came to power, and
the militant rise of the common man behind Andrew Jackson.
There was, of course, the Industrial Revolution, followed by the
heroic Populist Revolt; and similar social conflicts throughout
the Colonial period caught their attention. . . .

In contrast, the new look of American history is strikingly conservative. More than at any time before, historians are discovering
a placid, unexciting past. To an impressive degree, the dominant
interpretations have recaptured the spirit of Alexis de Tocqueville,
whose *Democracy in America* has emerged in recent years from a
characteristic neglect during the early 20th century. As Tocqueville
did more than a century ago, today's historians are exhibiting a
happy land, adventurous in manner but conservative in substance,
and—above all—remarkably homogeneous.

For one thing, current scholarship is carrying out a massive
grading operation to smooth over America's social convulsions.
The American Revolution has lost its revolutionary character,
becoming again what genteel historians had always said it was: a
reluctant resistance of sober Englishmen to infringements on
English liberties. We have learned that the Jacksonians yearned
nostalgically to restore the stable simplicity of a bygone age, and
that the Populists were rural businessmen deluded by a similar
pastoral mythology. . . .

Among earlier crises, the Civil War alone has resisted somewhat the flattening process. Yet a significant decline has occurred
in the number of important contributions to Civil War history
from professional scholars. One is tempted to conclude that dis-
turbances which cannot be minimized must be neglected. On
the other hand, the growing attraction of the Civil War to
journalists suggests that it provides a larger public with a kind
of surrogate for all of the other dramatic moments that historians
are deflating.

By reducing the importance of these turning points, the newer
interpretations have enabled us to rediscover the continuity of
American history, the stability of basic institutions, the tough-
ness of the social fabric. The same result is also being attained
by dissolving the persistent dualisms, which Parrington and Beard
emphasized, and substituting a monistic pattern. Instead of two

traditions or sections or classes deployed against one another all along the line of national development, we are told that America in the largest sense has had one unified culture. Classes have turned into myths, sections have lost their solidarity, ideologies have vaporized into climates of opinion. The phrase "*the* American experience" has become an incantation. . . .

Of course, the new interpreters have to face a considerable amount of real strife at various times in the history of the nation. They must also recognize that many Americans at such times have *thought* their country cleft between "haves" and "have-nots." But an emphasis on the belief can help to minimize the reality. A psychological approach to conflict enables historians to substitute a schism in the soul for a schism in society. Certainly present-day scholars tend to subjectivize the stresses in American life. Divisions, which the previous generation understood as basic opposition between distinct groups, turn into generalized psychological tensions running through the society as a whole. John Dos Passos's bitter outburst in the 1930's—"all right we are two nations"—becomes the record of a state of mind. An able synthesis of recent research on the age of the great tycoons explains the popular outcries against them as a projection upon one group of responsibility for the rapid industrial changes into which all were thrown.

Accordingly, when historians today write critically, they scrupulously avoid singling out any one segment of the population for blame. They either criticize the myths and stereotypes that have exaggerated the differences between competing groups; or they attack our uniformities and hanker for more variety. Louis Hartz, in what was perhaps the most outstanding of the new interpretive books, *The Liberal Tradition in America: An Interpretation of American Political Thought Since the Revolution* (1955), worried because we have no other tradition. A regime of freedom has had so unchallenged a sway in America, Hartz contended, that most American political debate has been shadow-boxing. "America must look to its contact with other nations to provide that spark of philosophy, that grain of relative insight that its own history has denied it."

Hartz's own sympathies lay with dissent and diversity. He was clearly disturbed by the soporific intellectual implications of the liberal consensus he described. To take full advantage of the new monolithic approach to American history would require a point of view much more complacent, much less internationally oriented, and much less respectful of the value of ideas. About the time when Hartz was first publishing the early chapters of his book in scholarly journals, Daniel J. Boorstin was making a similar but more drastic revision of American history in a conservative direction. Boorstin wrote in a mood thoroughly in tune with the unphilosophic harmony which he and Hartz were independently appraising.

A slim volume of lectures published in 1953, *The Genius of American Politics,* stated the essence of Boorstin's thesis. Ostensibly, the book concerned a relatively limited problem: why has America produced almost no systematic, fundamental political theory? Boorstin was not the first, of course, to brood over this question. Most American intellectual historians try pretty hard to deny the charge. Boorstin, however, had no apologies to make. He presented this supposed shortcoming as a triumphant demonstration of our success as a nation. With sour, sidelong glances at Europe, he argued that Americans did not need basic theories. Having no deep antagonisms, they could dispense with metaphysical defenses. Never having repudiated their past, they could discuss their problems as lawyers rather than political philosophers. American values had emerged from happy experience; here the "ought" derived from the "is." In the 20th century, he admitted, Americans could no longer take themselves for granted; but let them not therefore try to acquire an ideology and become crusaders. American political thought need only consult the wisdom imbedded in our historic institutions. In spite of the author's contempt for European theory, a bit of Edmund Burke proved useful in the end.

This celebration of the mindlessness of American life came from no provincial lowbrow. Boorstin is one of the very few native students of American history who possesses European culture, and participates in it with easy familiarity. A Rhodes Scholar, a student at various times of the humanities and the biological sciences, a barrister of the Inner Temple, author of a study in English intellectual history, he knows of what he scorns. Yet the view he advanced in *The Genius of American Politics* cannot be dismissed simply as an intellectual's self-hatred—the perversity of a man somehow driven to revulsion from what he has cherished. The book was more than this. It crisply summarized and foreshadowed the new trend of American historiography: the appeal to homogeneity, continuity, and national character. Above all, it swept aside the characteristically progressive approach to American intellectual history as a dialectic of warring ideologies.

Louis Hartz was already doing the same thing in the articles later reprinted in his *Liberal Tradition in America,* though Hartz's appraisal showed the intellectual deficiencies produced by the homogeneity and continuity of American society. Having no such qualms about our supposedly one-track culture, Boorstin went a step beyond Hartz. The latter at least conceded to America one system of ideas; Boorstin admitted none at all.

In their different but overlapping ways, the two books sketched the general outlines of an anti-progressive interpretation of American history. While other scholars were rewriting specific episodes in the story, Boorstin and Hartz revised the plot. Boorstin did not leave the matter there, however. He has now come forth with the first volume of a projected trilogy, ambitiously entitled *The Americans,* which brilliantly elaborates the thesis stated in his previous book. The new volume ranges lightly but learnedly across the Colonial period. Far from being confined to political forms, about which it says relatively little, it has sections on religion, science, the professions, styles of speech, the press, and the art of war. On each of these subjects Boorstin presses the central theme that America flourished by scrapping European blueprints, dissolving the social and intellectual distinctions of European life, and moving toward a homogeneous society of undifferentiated men. The whole work amounts to a running demonstration that a naive practicality enabled Americans from a very early date to unite in a stable way of life, undisturbed by divisive principles.

*   *   *

The author of *The Americans* did not always write with such affection for the expediential and such scorn for theories. In 1948 he published *The Lost World of Thomas Jefferson,* a searching examination of the structure and assumptions of Jeffersonian thought. In that book he took abstract principles very seriously indeed. There he explored the philosophical results of the American pragmatic temper—and found them dangerous. The main emphasis fell on Jefferson's undervaluing of the reflective side of human nature: "the desire to get things done predominated over the need to be at peace with God and oneself." This book maintained that Jefferson's distrust of metaphysics mired him in intellectual confusion, and that his materialistic premises led ultimately to the moral obtuseness of modern American thought. Now, through an extraordinary reversal, the vices imputed to Jefferson have become the virtues of America. With incredible virtuosity, Boorstin has furnished a new map of American history with each spin of his own intellectual compass.

To understand this about-face, it may help to note that both books have a deeply conservative character, though in different ways. *The Lost World* rests on a philosophical conservatism. It might almost have been written by a neo-Thomist, for essentially it accuses the liberal tradition, which stretches from Jefferson to Dewey, of lacking humility in the face of God and history. *The Americans,* on the other hand, grows out of an empirical conservatism, which rejects all ideologies in the name of long-established institutions. The earlier book implies that we need a conservative philosophy. The recent one tells us that we have something much better: a conservative way of life.

The shift from one position to the other reflects, I think, a change of fashion in conservative thinking. During the late 1940's and early 1950's a good many intellectuals with historical interests were trying to define a tradition of conservative thought in America. Historians had for so long canonized a succession of liberal heroes that the first reaction to the new postwar mood was to create a competing pantheon of conservative luminaries. Books by Russell Kirk, Clinton Rossiter, and other intellectual historians revealed that a number of American thinkers had respected original sin and had opposed the official cult of progress. Boorstin's *Lost World* fell in with this effort, though it contributed negatively by exposing the alleged failure of the liberal tradition.

Before long, however, the attempt to establish the value of a European type of conservatism in the American environment petered out; we hear very little of it today. The campaign had too obviously polemical a flavor and too unreal a taste: a tempest in an academic teapot. Great faith was required to believe that men like George Fitzhugh, Orestes Brownson, and Irving Babbitt ever had much profundity or any considerable impact. The really massive conservatism of American businessmen, politicians, and even most intellectuals, as we were discovering, spoke in the common language of the Enlightenment. Liberals and conservatives no longer seemed clearly distinguishable. As the ideological gap between them appeared to shrink, and as a mood of acquiescence spread in all quarters, the need to vindicate a conservative intellectual tradition disappeared. When the liberal ideology lost its cutting edge, conservatives ceased to require an ideological shield.

At this point a historiography that was conservative, without passing as such, won out. Instead of upholding the role of the right in America, it merges the left with the right. It argues that America has ordinarily fused a conservative temper with a liberal state of mind. It displays, therefore, the homogeneity and the continuity of American culture. Writing sympathetically about the intellectual conservatism of today, Eric McKitrick has recently pointed out that it stresses the power of institutions; it has no ideological case to make—except, one might add, a case against ideologies. Boorstin, in his last two books, has joined this school, and, in a sense, has taken the lead.

The advantages of this point of view for American historians have not been slight. It has enabled them to cut through the too easy dualisms of progressive historiography. It is inspiring them to do important and original work in understanding American institutions. They should continue to do so. The conservative frame of reference, however, creates a paralyzing incapacity to deal with the elements of spontaneity, effervescence, and violence in American history. Richard Chase, one of the few literary critics who has successfully defied the current mood, has recently called attention to the wildness and extravagance that characterized the outstanding American novels. Similar qualities have shaken our society, from the Great Awakening of the 18th century to the Great Red Scares of the 20th, in spite of its sturdy institutional structure. They deserve more than patronizing attention.

Moreover, contemporary conservatism has a deadening effect on the historian's ability to take a conflict of ideas seriously. Either he disbelieves in the conflict itself (Americans having been pretty much of one mind), or he trivializes it into a set of psychological adjustments to institutional change. In either case, the current fog of complacency, flecked with anxiety, spreads backward over the American past.

It is not likely in the near future that many critical scholars will emphasize the polarities that fascinated the great progressive historians, nor is it desirable that they should. Certainly no one contends today that the debate between Jefferson and Hamilton, or between human rights and property rights, frames our intellectual history. But to stand Parrington and Beard on their heads does not solve the problem. American thought has had other dialectical patterns, which the present cult of consensus hides. Above all, perhaps, that cult neutralizes some moral issues that have played a not entirely petty or ignoble part in the history of the United States. To rediscover their grandeur and urgency, historians do not need the categories of Beard and Parrington, and can probably do without their now debased pragmatic philosophy. But we pay a cruel price in dispensing with their deeper values: an appreciation of the crusading spirit, a responsiveness to indignation, a sense of injustice.

ROBERT A. DAHL

American Political Institutions and the Resolution of Conflict

Robert Dahl, Sterling Professor of Political Science at Yale University, was President of the American Political Science Association in 1966–1967. References to his many publications are to be found in the "Suggestions for Additional Reading" at the end of this volume. In the following selection from his latest book, Dahl, while acknowledging that the "normal" condition of American politics is one of moderate conflict, points out that regularly in every generation the American system has been called upon to cope with conflicts of extreme severity. Furthermore, he raises an interesting doubt as to whether a system geared to handling moderate conflict is equally well suited to the resolution of severe conflict.

IT IS OFTEN SUPPOSED, not only by foreigners but by Americans themselves, that except for the one Civil War the American political system has managed to avoid severe conflicts. Americans, it is often said, are a moderate people; they display their moderation even in their conflicts, most of all in their political conflicts. How much truth does this view contain?

. . . If one accepts as signs of the severity of a conflict such indicators as threats or moves to disrupt the constitutional system, or threatened or actual violence against or on behalf of national policies, or expressions by sober and informed observers, or participants that a given conflict will lead to disruption, revolution, or civil war—if one accepts these as portents, then the weight of historical evidence does seem to offer solid support to this proposition: From the very first years under the new Constitution, American political life has undergone *about once every generation* a conflict over national politics of *extreme severity.* . . .

To suggest the evidence for this proposition, let me review some familiar historical episodes.

Before the Constitution had completed its first decade, the Alien and Sedition Acts (1798)—which threatened the very existence of any organized political opposition—were challenged by the legislatures of Kentucky (1798) and Virginia (1799) in resolutions that hinted for the first time (but definitely not the last) that a state government might deliberately refuse to enforce a federal law which its legislators held to be unconstitutional. The specters raised by the Alien and Sedition Acts on the one side, and by the Kentucky and Virginia resolutions on the other, were temporarily banished by what Jefferson called "the Revolution of 1800."

Within hardly more than another decade, New England Federalists, driven to desperation by the embargo policies enforced by the Republicans, assembled at Hartford (December, 1814) in a convention that not only adopted a set of resolutions calling for extensive constitutional changes but issued a report asserting among other things that "in cases of deliberate, dangerous, and palpable infraction of the Constitution, affecting the sovereignty of a State and liberties of the people; it is not only the right but the duty of such a State to interpose its authority for their protection, in the manner best calculated to secure that end."

Less than another score of years went by before the United
States approached civil war over the tariff. In 1828, the legislature
of South Carolina adopted a set of eight resolutions holding the
newly passed "Tariff of Abominations," which ultimately hit cotton exporters with what seemed to them undue harshness, unconstitutional, oppressive, and unjust; in an accompanying document
written by John C. Calhoun the legislature espoused the view that
in such cases a single state might "nullify" an unconstitutional
law (1828). Four years later when the South Carolinians were still
chafing under the protective tariff, a convention called by the state
legislature adopted an ordinance that "nullified" the tariff acts of
1828 and 1832, prohibited the collection of duties within the state,
and asserted that the use of force by the federal government could
be cause for secession. The state legislature passed laws to enforce
the ordinance, to raise a military force, and to appropriate funds
for arms. President Jackson thereupon sought and gained from
Congress the legal authority to enforce the tariff laws, by military
means, if necessary. A compromise tariff was worked out in Congress, South Carolina rescinded her Ordinance of Nullification,
and civil war was avoided—or rather postponed for thirty years.

Thereafter, the middle years of the century were occupied with
various aspects of the controversy over slavery, particularly whether
slavery should be permitted in the great unsettled areas of the
West, a question that touched the most sensitive interests of North-
erners and Southerners. Finally, as everyone knows, the issue no
longer could be contained; and for four terrible years men died of
wounds and disease to settle the question—or so it was supposed.

Although it does not quite fit in our list of severe conflicts, there
occurred in the decade before the Civil War a curious political
phenomenon that is worth remarking. In the 1840s European im-
migration, chiefly from Ireland and Germany, greatly increased.
A nativistic, anti-foreign, anti-Catholic, super-patriotic reaction began to set in. In the early fifties, political tickets consisting of anti-
foreign candidates appeared in New York, Pennsylvania, and New
Jersey. Soon a party began organizing secretly; it called itself the
American party; because its members refused to divulge their
secrets, their enemies called them Know Nothings. The party
showed some promise of replacing the Whig Party. As it turned
out, however, the life of the American party was brief and unsuc-
cessful, for it was consumed in the struggle over slavery. Had it

prospered, the whole course of American history would have been different.

The issue of slavery was settled only in part by the Civil War: slavery was abolished, to be sure, but the freed Negroes were not long permitted to enjoy equal political rights—to say nothing of economic, educational, or social privileges. Ten years after Appomattox, the election of 1876 brought the country to the verge of civil war, but as so often before and after, the outcome was compromise rather than war; yet a compromise that tacitly allowed the restoration of White Supremacy throughout the South and thus adjourned the whole problem of effective citizenship for Negroes until the middle of the present century.

This adjournment allowed economic questions to take over. During the last third of the century, discontented farmers and urban workers formed a pool of recurring opposition to the policies of a national government which responded less and less to their demands than to those of the new men of business, industry, and finance. Out of economic dissatisfaction, radical and reformist movements developed: Socialist Labor, the Greenbackers, the Farmers' Alliance, Populism, the Socialist Party, the IWW. The trade union movement also had its turbulent beginnings: the Knights of Labor, the AFL, the railway unions. Strikes, lockouts, and protest meetings frequently led to severe violence.

In the presidential elections of 1896, William Jennings Bryan, a man of primitive intellect and beguiling eloquence, whom Democrats and Populists had jointly nominated as their candidate, and who in his simple and confused protests against the "domination of Eastern Capital," evidently evoked support among a considerable number of farmers and some urban workers, was defeated by McKinley after a campaign period of unusually high tension.

Sixteen years later, a new Democratic President, the second since the Civil War, was elected; under Wilson's leadership many of the specific reforms that had been demanded earlier by Populists and Socialists were carried out. Although these reforms were sharply opposed, the conflicts seem to have lacked some of the earlier intensity; the country was not widely viewed as approaching another civil war.

The next generation witnessed the Great Depression, mass unemployment, extensive discontent, the election of the third Democratic President since the Civil War, new outbreaks of violence, the rise of quasi-democratic or anti-democratic political movements on both right and left, and extensive changes in national policies, changes that from 1935 onward were fought with increasing bitterness. Driven to extreme measures by a Supreme Court dominated by conservatives who steadily rejected the major items of the New Deal as unconstitutional, President Roosevelt in 1937 even tried to "pack" the Court. It was his first important move to prove unpopular, and he was defeated. From about 1937 until the bombing of Pearl Harbor in 1941, political leaders were bitterly divided over the question whether it was better to meet threats of military aggression by "isolation" or "intervention."

Less than thirty years later, the unsolved problem of equal rights and opportunities for Negroes produced a new eruption of demonstrations, discontent, and violence—not only in the South but also in the Negro ghettos of the large Northern cities. And in 1964 the long-frustrated opposition of the radical right, capitalizing on white reactions to Negro discontent, temporarily captured the Republican Party and at last found national spokesmen in the Republican nominees for President and Vice President, Senator Goldwater and Representative Miller.

Whoever supposes, then, that American politics has been nothing more than a moving consensus, a sort of national Rotary Club luncheon, has not sufficiently reflected on the regularity of intense conflict, crisis, and violence in American history.

*   *   *

In times of moderate conflict, American political institutions encourage compromise, consensual decisions, and incremental changes. But what is the effect of the political institutions when proposals for more comprehensive changes inspire severe conflicts? Political institutions continue to provide stubborn and well organized groups numerous opportunities to veto, modify, or delay the passage or enforcement of policies that would entail comprehensive change. Hence even in the face of proposals for more far-reaching changes, and even in the presence of increasingly severe conflict, the tendency of the political institutions is to handle severe conflicts along the same lines as moderate conflicts. American political institutions, then, encourage political leaders to respond to severe conflicts in three ways:

1. By forming a new political coalition that can overpower the opposition. But this, as we shall see, is a difficult solution.
2. By incremental measures that postpone comprehensive change.
3. By enduring compromises that remove the issue from serious political conflict.

Overpowering the Opposition

A severe conflict is sometimes moderated or even terminated when one political coalition gains enough power to overcome the resistance of its opponents. Instead of compromising, the winning coalition enacts its policies despite the opposition of the defeated coalition. If the opposition fights back, as it is likely to do, it finds itself too weak to prevail. Unable to reverse the main direction of policy imposed by the winning coalition, the opposition may in time accept the major policies enacted by the winners and settle down to bargaining for incremental adjustments; thus severe conflict gives way to a period of moderate conflict.

Probably the only effective way in American politics for one coalition significantly to reduce the bargaining power of an enemy coalition is to turn it into a visible and even isolated political minority by defeating it in national elections. However, because of the large number of positions where an embattled minority, unable to win the Presidency or a majority in either house of Congress, can dig in and successfully continue to challenge the policies of the majority coalition, a single electoral victory is ordinarily not necessarily enough, particularly if the contest is close. The victories of the winning coalition may have to be large, thus visibly demonstrating the weakness of the opposition, and repeated in a series of presidential and congressional elections, thus demonstrating for all to see that the minority coalition has little chance of regaining its power and must come to terms with the victors.

In at least three instances, severe conflicts seem to have been moderated or terminated in this way:

1. After Republicans overwhelmed Federalists in the elections of 1800 and continued to do so for a generation. By 1814 when the Federalists at the Hartford Convention talked disunion, their leaders gained little national support. After 1814 Federalism dis-

appeared as an effective political movement, though old Federalist leaders constituted a kind of feeble opposition until they died or despaired.

2. From the mid-term elections of 1894 onward, and particularly after the presidential election of 1896 when Republicans over-whelmed the coalition of Democrats and Populists that supported William Jennings Bryan and thereby moderated (and postponed) a severe conflict over economic policies. The defeat of the Populists meant that neither of the two major parties would develop into a farmer-labor coalition with an ideology and program comparable to those of the British and European Labor and Socialist parties. A major challenge to unregulated capitalism was turned back and a socialist alternative was effectively removed from American political competition. . . .

3. After 1932 when elections temporarily destroyed the power of the Republican coalition centered on the policies of business and thereby made it possible for most of the New Deal proposals of FDR to be enacted. By the time the Republican opposition was able to regroup, it could no longer *undo* the New Deal except in minor ways. However, it entered into a coalition with Southern Democrats, which by bargaining in Congress impeded or prevented further reforms until the power of both the Republicans and the Southern Democrats was temporarily smashed by the presidential and congressional elections of 1964.

Yet elections are often indecisive; neither Truman's re-election in 1948 nor Kennedy's election in 1960 enabled the victorious President to enact the major policies he and his party had advo-cated in the campaign, despite the fact that both Presidents had Democratic majorities in Congress. Truman presented to Congress an extensive Fair Deal program involving a number of social re-forms. But only a few of these had been enacted when he went out of office. Why are elections so infrequently decisive? Why, people often ask, don't elections settle things one way or the other? Why is it so difficult for a President and Congress ostensibly of the same party to terminate a severe conflict by over-riding the objec-tions of their opponents, carrying through their legislative program, and letting the country decide at the next election whether it likes the changes or disapproves of them?

By now it must be clear to the reader that American political institutions were never designed to operate in this fashion; nor do they. But in addition to the institutions themselves, several aspects of American beliefs, sentiments, or loyalties reduce still further the likelihood that elections can be decisive. For one thing party loyalties are, as we have seen, incredibly persistent. It is uncomfortably close to being true that either of the two major parties could probably win twenty million votes for its presidential candidate even if it nominated Ed the Talking Horse. The overwhelming electoral sweeps in the presidential elections of 1936, 1952, and 1964 left the defeated minority with a substantial share of popular votes (37 per cent in 1936, 44 per cent in 1952, 39 per cent in 1964). In the twenty-six presidential elections from 1864–1964, the defeated party received less than 40 per cent only seven times; it received 45 per cent or more in twelve elections, and from 40–45 per cent seven times. A party overwhelmed by a landslide is far indeed from being in a hopeless situation.

Then, too, the votes of a winning coalition are not uniformly distributed throughout the country; there are sizeable regional variations. A political minority in the nation may be a political majority in a region, as with the New England Federalists in 1800 or the Democrats in the South in every election won by a Republican President from 1860 onward. A defeated minority with a powerful regional base stands a good chance not only of surviving but of keeping most of its senior political leaders in Congress. . . .

Since the earliest times, doctrines of unalterable rights and of states' rights have both been invoked by defeated minorities to challenge the legitimacy or constitutionality of laws enacted or proposed by President and Congress. Attacks on national law in the name of the rights of individuals or states or both were expressed in the Virginia and Kentucky Resolutions of 1798–99, the declaration of the Hartford Convention in 1814, the South Carolina Resolutions in 1828, the "Exposition and Protest" accompanying them, the Ordinance of Nullification in 1832, and South Carolina's "Declaration of the Cause of Secession" in December, 1860. These principles were revived in the South from 1954 onward as the doctrine of "interposition" to justify resistance to the Supreme Court's decisions on integration.

American political institutions, then, do not ordinarily endow the candidates or parties who receive a majority of votes in an election with enough power to carry out their policies over the opposition of the defeated minority. And American political beliefs do not endow the winning majority with over-arching and unambiguous legitimacy; nor do they deprive the defeated minority of grounds on which to argue that its policies and not those of the majority must be allowed to prevail.

Consequently, while a severe conflict is sometimes terminated by an overwhelming victory for one side in a congressional and presidential election, the American political system and American beliefs make this solution somewhat difficult and uncommon.

Postponing Comprehensive Changes

American political institutions are excellently designed for making incremental changes. But they also foster delay in coming to grips with questions that threaten severe conflict. It is true that delay may provide precious time during which a seemingly severe problem may change its shape, becoming more manageable, even disappear. But postponement may also inhibit leaders from facing a problem squarely and searching for decisive solutions—solutions that may be forced upon them many years later when they can no longer delay.

Policies of economic reform which were barely more than marginal have sometimes taken decades or even generations to accomplish. When the Democrats won the Presidency and majorities in the Congress in 1892 that enabled them to pass an income tax law, the Supreme Court, rightly foreseeing that the income tax could be the foundation for redistribution at the expense of the rich, struck it down; it required sixteen years and the Sixteenth Amendment to make it possible for Congress to enact an income tax again. The regulation of child labor . . . was held up for a generation by a Supreme Court unwilling to yield to Congress and President. In 1948, President Truman, acting on recommendations from his advisory Committee on Civil Rights, recommended federal legislation against lynching, the poll-tax, segregation in public transportation, and discrimination in employment. Although mild civil rights legislation was passed in 1957 and 1960, no major legislation on civil rights cleared Congress until 1964, almost two decades after President Truman's recommendations. Passage of American welfare and social security laws has followed the enactment of comparable laws in most European democracies by one to several generations. A national medical care program has been advocated for generations. In 1945, President Truman proposed to a Congress a comprehensive medical insurance program for persons of all ages. The first law establishing a national system of medical insurance, though only for the elderly, was not enacted until 1965.

Compromise

The existence of innumerable fortified positions from which an embattled but well organized minority can fight off and wear down an attack, combined with the absence of any *single* rule for making legitimate decisions on which the political activists are agreed, means that it is difficult to terminate a conflict by the clear-cut victory of one side over another. Hence severe conflicts are sometimes handled by reaching a compromise. Occasionally the result is a long-lasting compromise. Two of the most enduring compromises of this kind in American history both involved the Negro; both sought to eliminate the Negro as a source of severe conflict among Whites; both succeeded in doing so for long periods; both were at the expense of the Negro; and by present-day standards in all civilized countries, both were unjust. One dealt with the Negro as slave, the other with the Negro as freed slave.

The first was the Missouri Compromise of 1820 which, by providing that slavery would be permitted south but not north of the line 36° 30′ across the vast territory acquired in the Louisiana Purchase, promised to maintain a balance between the numbers of free and slave states and thereby preserve to each side a veto over future national policies. This compromise kept the problem of slavery in the territories and the future of slavery itself within manageable bounds for thirty years. Then the new land acquired as a result of the Mexican war added territories not covered by the old compromise and . . . triggered off the decade of severe conflict that eventuated in the Civil War.

The second great compromise was arrived at in 1877, after the long crisis produced by the contested presidential election of 1876. . . . Briefly, however, the effect of this settlement was to bury Reconstruction and to permit white Southerners to restore White Supremacy. Once again the fate of the Negro was removed as a source of severe conflict—once again by Whites at Negro expense. This shameful compromise endured for seventy years. The beginning of the end for the compromise of 1877 was legislation mentioned a moment ago on civil rights and employment introduced by President Truman. His proposals split the Democratic party and strengthened the coalition of Southern Democrats and Northern Republicans in Congress; hence it was not until the passage of the Civil Rights Acts of 1964 and 1965 that the Compromise of 1877 came finally to an end.

These two experiences say something about the limits of compromise. First, there are moral limits; by the standards of the con-

temporary civilized world, both of our great national compromises
went beyond these limits. Second, it is obvious that one necessary
condition for any such compromise is that the contestants can
somehow discover an alternative that vastly reduces the threat
from the other side, particularly by eliminating or markedly decreasing the dangers to the way of life defended by one or more
contestants. Such a solution may not exist, or—what amounts to
pretty much the same thing—it may not be discovered. The Compromises of 1820 and 1877 were possible only because Negroes
had no voice in arranging them. If spokesmen for the slaves had
enjoyed the same veto power over national policies that spokesmen for slaveholders possessed until 1860, the Compromise of
1820 would have been impossible. If the freedman had been as
influential in 1877 as white Southerners that compromise too would
have been impossible.

A Tentative Conclusion

One effect of all these factors is to impede decisive action through
the ordinary processes of presidential leadership and congressional
law-making. The consequences of this are two-fold and not lacking in paradox. The system encourages Presidents who wish to be
decisive to draw on their reservoir of powers that lie outside the
control of Congress or Courts; hence in these domains, most visibly
in foreign policy, the President is more and more his own master
and the normal processes are more and more displaced by executive decision. Yet side by side with presidential decisiveness in
areas where he cannot be closely controlled, the system operates
to inhibit decisive action. Thus while incremental changes can be
bargained for, large reforms that elsewhere have been enacted in
a single session of parliament hard on the heels of a single election must in the United States await many elections and many sessions of Congress. To make the point once more, the system encourages incremental change; it discourages comprehensive change.
It facilitates the negotiation of moderate conflicts.

But what is the effect of American political institutions on severe
conflict? Do they intensify conflict by preventing early if drastic
changes in policies? Do they prolong and exacerbate severe conflict? Although the evidence we have examined in this chapter
lends itself to this interpretation, one must confess that the evidence
is murky and allows a different argument. Yet it would be hard
to deny that the danger is there.

II Environment or Inheritance

RAY ALLEN BILLINGTON

Frontier Democracy

Ray Allen Billington, formerly William Smith Mason Professor of History at Northwestern University, is currently Senior Research Associate at the Huntington Library. Among his works are The Protestant Crusade (*1938*); Westward Expansion (*1949*); *and* The Far Western Frontier, 1830–1860 (*1956*). *This selection from his most recent book,* The Frontier Heritage (*1966*), *supports Frederick Jackson Turner's frontier thesis with reasonableness and impressive scholarship.*

"AMERICAN DEMOCRACY," wrote Frederick Jackson Turner, "was born of no theorist's dream; it was not carried in the *Sarah Constant* [*sic*] to Virginia, nor in the *Mayflower* to Plymouth. It came out of the American forest, and it gained new strength each time it touched a new frontier." This simple statement has been more vigorously attacked than any other penned by Turner. Nonsense, cried the critics. Well-developed democratic theories and institutions *were* carried to America by the colonists. Within the New World the settled Easts contributed more to democratic practices— manhood suffrage, the secret ballot, equal representation—than the retreating Wests. Here was Turner at his worst, guilty not only of distortion but of positive untruth.

Were those critics right? Perhaps an answer to that question can be found by examining their arguments. These may be grouped into four general propositions: the frontier failed to alter the anti-democratic behavior of those who fell under its influence; it was a region of conservatism rather than of liberalism; political and social reforms originated in the East rather than the West; and the pioneers were imitative rather than creative in their political behavior, copying Eastern constitutions when they formed their states, and lagging rather than leading in the introduction of manhood suffrage.

*   *   *

How valid were these arguments? We can grapple with that question only after making clear that we are discussing not democracy but *American* democracy, as was Frederick Jackson Turner when he made his oft-disputed statement. Our discussion is based on the premise that there is a slight distinction between both the theory and the practice of democracy in the United States and Europe. This does not imply that America's debt to the Old World was insignificant; from England it borrowed the common law, a system of local government, a belief in a government of laws and not of men, and a variety of practices in representative government; from France it accepted the philosophy and example of a revolution that provided constitution makers with ringing phrases for generations to come. Europe also contributed the concept of man's right to choose his own means of salvation, a product of the Protestant Reformation and an essential plank in any democratic platform. That democracy did thrive in the Anglo-American portions of the New World was due primarily to this inheritance, which Spanish-America and French-America lacked.

American democracy differs from European in several ways. One is the relative lack of acknowledged class lines and the acceptance of each individual on his own merits. The freedom of every person to shape his own destiny, whatever his lineage, has been translated politically into an enduring faith in the "common man"—into the belief that the plain people are worthy of equality, freedom, and a share in the government. Sure of himself and his destiny, the American more than the European views the government as *his* property, to be used or changed as he sees fit. He has, to an unusual degree, a manipulative attitude toward both his constitution and elected officials; leadership must come not from the elite few but from the ordinary many. A nation in which the taxi driver addresses the governor of his state as "Mac" may be no more democratic than England or France, but the nature of the democracy is different.

American political faith deviates from the European in its emphasis on the inevitability of change. People in the Old World, burdened by their medieval heritage and shackled by traditionalism, are less inclined to look upon progress as the normal state of affairs. They view governmental institutions as solidified, changeable only by violence. Americans are calmly confident that peaceful means will be found to solve the most complex problems, and certain that democratic practices will eventually bring peace and prosperity to all. Their abhorrence of violence is shared by the English, but not their faith in progress. This belief has allowed political institutions to evolve without the disorders that have marked change in many European nations.

Finally, there is a freshness in the American political atmosphere that has struck visitors to the nation's shores from the eighteenth century to the present. Observers have found in the lifted head of the American woman, the persistent ability of chance acquaintances to pry into the personal details of one's life, the universal faith in the infallibility of the majority, the dislike of privilege and the privileged, the aloof indifference of waiters to the needs of their customers, the surly independence of taxicab drivers, the eagerness of parents to cater to the whims of their children, the annoying habit of engaging strangers in conversation, the tendency to fasten nicknames on governmental officials, and the insistence on equal opportunity for all, evidence that the American environment did add something to democratic theories and practices imported from abroad. This "something" is not measurable by empirical techniques, nor capable of reduction to statistical tables, but too many generations of Europeans visiting America and Americans visiting Europe have testified to its existence to dispute its reality.

The differences that distinguish American from European democracy are traceable to a complex of forces, but our concern is with only one of these: the influence of three centuries of frontiering. Over the course of many years both visitors from abroad and students of the local scene have suggested a variety of means whereby the pioneering experience altered democratic theories and practices in the United States. The frontier, they argue, affected these changes by providing opportunity for individual betterment

and a corresponding dislike of external rule, by serving as a leveling force that lessened the economic gulf between peoples, by altering the power structure and opening the door for new leadership,
by creating a social atmosphere scornful of tradition where experimentation in institutional forms was acceptable, and by allowing
repeated experiments as frontiersmen rebuilt their governments on
successive frontiers. These five arguments must be examined before
we test their validity against the actual history of democratic
change on the frontier.

The opportunity for individual self-betterment provided by
abundant natural resources in successive wests, and the even more
important belief that opportunity was open to all, radically altered
the pioneers' attitude toward government. In America all men
could acquire the possessions that stood for privilege in older
countries; why then should not all men share equally in control
of the state? "The price of land," wrote a Westerner, "is the ther-
mometer of liberty—men are freest where lands are cheapest."
Alexis de Tocqueville, one of the shrewdest of all European observers, believed that God had assured freedom for the Americans
by placing them in a boundless continent where they needed only
to shift to the frontiers to secure the material basis for equality.
No man, no matter how poor, would bow before a landed gentry
when he was confident that he would one day possess estates of
his own. The frontier elite might think of themselves as the "better
sort," but their less fortunate neighbors refused to admit that
"betters" existed. So long as economic equality was within reach,
political equality was its inevitable by-product.

The frontier also fostered a unique type of American democracy
by serving as a leveling force that minimized traditional differences between men. This occurred partly as a result of the sifting
process that kept the very rich and the very poor from migrating;
the wealthy, an Englishman on the Ohio frontier noted, "were de-
terred by the difficulties attending a new settlement; the indigent
by the impossibility of getting vacant lands." In the West equality
of opportunity continued to lessen class distinctions, and to de-
preciate the importance of inherited status, social prestige, or correct lineage. Tocqueville insisted that belief in equality was the
key to understanding the people of the United States, the "fundamental fact from which all others seem to be derived." He recognized also that this attitude had been nurtured by the social environment of the frontier, where the principle of egalitarianism was

so enshrined that a candidate could succeed politically only by pretending to be of, not above, the common people. . . .

Even more important was the frontier's role as a catalyst in altering the leadership structure within pioneer communities. In established societies with long-functioning power structures, apathy and a tendency to trust those in control tended to concentrate governmental functions in the hands of certain classes, groups, or families, thus closing the door to outsiders. No such structure existed in the new communities of the West. Those who could convince their neighbors that they possessed certain qualities—energy and ability, identification with the interests of the people, readiness to follow instructions from below—were able to achieve political power, whatever their backgrounds. Leadership is normally entrusted to those who best live up to the standard of behavior valued by the group. On new frontiers, there was every opportunity for those persons to sort themselves out, even though they had played no similar roles before. This was a powerful democratizing influence.

As this sifting went on, certain qualities emerged as valuable in pioneer communities. The frontiersmen wanted leaders who lived as they lived, and thought as they thought. "The successful politician," wrote one of the most observing visitors to the frontier, "in a new country, where deference for experience or culture has not yet grown up, is, after all, the man who has most facility in expressing the ideas which are filling the heads of his neighbors." He must be a man abundantly possessed of the attributes essential in pioneer life, and above all he must appeal to the voters as an equal rather than as a superior. They wanted a candidate who (as one put it) "ain't too darn'd proud to shake hands with a poor man." A prospective office holder who campaigned by singing songs, winking at the spectators, and eating an onion in one hand and corn pone with the other . . . might not be setting high standards of political morality, but he was proving himself a real representative of the people. The willingness of Westerners to elect such men opened wide the door of opportunity to many who would have been barred from office in the East.

Such extreme political demagoguery was far from typical, for while the power structure was altered by the social environment of the frontier, the pioneers instinctively elevated men of proved ability and usually of affluence to posts of command. This had been their political habit for generations, and it was too strong to be broken. Yet in doing so, they transferred power from the well-born to the men "who are in fact the generals of the great migration," as an able observer noted. They shifted authority from the territorial governor inflicted on them from the East, and gave it to the local magistrate who might have been a teamster or a steamboat captain or a lawyer before his elevation to office. They normally chose as their leaders merchants and professional men who had proved themselves by achieving economic and social success in their new homes; very often in pioneer communities they entrusted authority to the little band of Freemasons who formed a cohesive elite group among the first settlers. But these were merchants and professional men attuned to the Western scene and fitted to grapple with the problems of Western life. Such changes in leadership certainly altered the nature of democracy.

This new type of leader was acceptable because in the West the dead hand of political tradition weighed less strongly on the people. Lacking a feudal heritage, and disdainful of even the recent past as a proper guide to life in a new land, the pioneers lacked the sense of political continuity that tended to perpetuate practices or group controls in older societies. They were freer to experiment, and bolder in their experimentation. In the Western states, Alexis de Tocqueville observed, "the inhabitants are but of yesterday," and so have "escaped the influence not only of great names and great wealth, but even of the natural aristocracy of knowledge and virtue." This rebellion against traditionalism was intensified by resentment against the immediate past; frontiersmen were certain that the East— whether symbolized by England's parliament in the case of the Virginia Company or by Washington's congress to the Californians —was too stultified to comprehend or solve their unique problems. The recurring demands for self-determination sharpened the Westerners' interest in government, and deepened their faith in democracy as an instrument for man's use.

Finally, an American brand of democracy was fostered by the recurring rebirth of government as the frontier advanced westward. "The western states of America," wrote a visitor, "are each a nursery of freedom: every new settlement is already a republic *in embryo.*" From the seventeenth century on, new governments were continuously born along the fringes of settlement, whether a Virginia House of Burgesses, or an assembly of the Watauga Association, or a new state in the Rocky Mountain country. Each meant an opportunity for experimentation, for adjustment to new conditions, for the introduction of democratic practices. Insomuch as most of these governments were formed in the late eighteenth and nineteenth centuries when the area of self-rule was expanding throughout the whole western world, Westerners were able to adopt reforms being tried elsewhere and adapt them to their own needs. This was important, for the frontier was not an area of political innovation; its contribution was to imitate and apply the democratic theories emerging in Europe and the East. In this fashion, no less than in others, it gave its stamp to a uniquely American form of democracy.

These explanations of the frontier's role in fostering an *American* democracy have the ring of truth about them, but it must be noted that they rest only on the observations of a few travelers and the theorizing of even fewer scholars. They can be substantiated only if put to the test of historical application. Was the frontier a catalyst inducing democratic change? Did it operate as a laboratory where liberal theories were tested, sorted, and utilized?

*   *   *

Both Kentucky and Tennessee drafted their first constitutions while dominated by a planter leadership imported from their mother states, Virginia and North Carolina, but government making in the Old Northwest suffered no such handicap. There existed an unusual opportunity for pioneer democracy to thrive uncontested. The population was remarkably homogeneous in economic and social status, yet recruited from such a variety of backgrounds that no built-in leadership group existed. Within the Old Northwest few farms surpassed 250 acres, which meant that no land holding elite had developed and the governing group must be drafted from the mass of the people. Those who gained power were men sufficiently able, and sufficiently glib of tongue, to convince the voters that they represented the popular will. Even more important was the widespread interest in politics, for the region was acutely conscious of its needs and aware that only vigorous leaders could supply them. Prosperity and future growth depended on more liberal land laws, better roads, protection against Indians, and a dozen other things needed on most frontiers. Officeholders who could work toward these ends, on both local and national levels, were essential.

This atmosphere endowed leadership posts with a status that made them eagerly sought after by capable and ambitious young men; it also led to an extraordinarily high level of political participation. "Everybody," wrote an Indiana settler, "expected at some time to be a candidate for something; or that his uncle would be; or his cousin, or his cousin's wife's cousin's friend would be; so that every body and every body's relations's friends were for ever electioneering." One Ohio county produced no less than ninety-four candidates for the ten posts allotted it in the constitutional convention of 1802. With this vying for office, and with the lively public interest in seeing that the right men were chosen, politics electrified the atmosphere months before each election. Every militia muster, every cabin raising or shooting match or log rolling, every Fourth of July celebration, was converted into a political convention as rival candidates stated their claims, bought drinks, and kissed babies. These pioneers were determined to select capable leaders who understood their wishes. Any politician who could demonstrate his ability to represent them would win their favor, whatever his prior status or lineage. Here was an ideal breeding ground for democratic practices.

Yet such is human nature that the restraints on self-rule normal in established societies appeared in the Old Northwest, although in modified form. While no planter class served as a brake on the popular will, a new elite of land speculators, merchants, and professional men in every new community arrayed themselves against mass control of the government. Human lethargy also played its part, especially in the constitution-drafting process, for mankind instinctively trusts the tested rather than the untested; delegates to conventions often adopted accepted devices used in Eastern states rather than more democratic practices of their own invention. These dual pressures—of propertied interests distrustful of popular control and of tradition-minded men apprehensive of experimentation—meant that the state constitutions drafted in the Ohio Valley would be imitative rather than creative, that they would reflect compromises essential in reconciling conflicts between contending factions, and that they would not automatically enshrine the democracy that was the faith of a majority of the people.

Given these conditions, the results were predictable. Only 11 of the 106 clauses of the Ohio Constitution of 1802 were original, only 21 of the 129 in the Indiana constitution of 1816, and only 15 of the 98 in the Illinois constitution of 1818. The remainder were copied from constitutions of Eastern or neighboring states, with an increasing tendency to rely on examples from near at hand. This practice meant that democratic innovation was slight on the Ohio Valley frontier, but it emphatically did *not* mean that democratic gains were not registered there. The tendency of constitution makers was to copy sections of other documents that mirrored their own philosophy, and to write new ones only when a satisfactory example could not be found. They selected from older frames of government the most democratic features, and welded them into documents that were surprisingly liberal for that day. Ohio opened its ballot box to all who paid any tax or had contributed work on the roads; Indiana and Illinois adopted manhood suffrage. Supreme power in all states was vested in a popularly elected legislature, whose members were rotated frequently, and in Ohio and Illinois the legislatures were unrestrained by any veto power on the part of the governor. Even judges were elected in Ohio for short terms, so that the courts would reflect the popular will. So insistent was the demand for election of officials, reported a cynical New Englander from Indiana, that every office was in control of the people from the governor's down to fence-viewer's clerk's assistants, and some wanted to let the electorate choose schoolteachers and professors at the state university.

In the other states of the Old Northwest and beyond the Mississippi the story was the same, for the pattern of state making was established in the Ohio Valley and varied little thereafter. Manhood suffrage was the universal rule, usually granted after residence in the state of six months or a year. Legislative powers were broad at first, then temporarily restricted in constitutions adopted immediately after the Panic of 1819, for the misrule that helped precipitate that financial debacle made the people distrustful of unrestrained popular control over property rights. They responded by writing longer and longer constitutions that themselves served as laws, or by limiting the functions and authority of assemblies while increasing those of governors. This setback was short lived; in 1844 Iowans rejected a constitution judged insufficiently republican and accepted another two years later when convinced that it gave adequate powers to the legislature. In general, constitution making throughout the West revealed faith in democracy and in the relatively unrestrained right of the peoples' elected representatives to govern.

On the level of local government the trend toward democratic practices was equally apparent. In the Old Northwest, the first charters inflicted on towns were patent-office models of those used in the East, for the rural-dominated legislatures had little concern with urban affairs. These undemocratic instruments, most of them restricting the suffrage and entrusting the mayor with excessive power, were short lived. During the 1830's and 1840's they were revolutionized to abolish property qualifications for voting and office holding, and to shift authority to elected councils. In Milwaukee a suggestion that aldermen hold office for three years was shouted down as "placing them beyond the reach of public opinion for a time almost equal to an age in older communities." Rotation in office was adopted with such enthusiasm that the mayors became mere figureheads, drawing no salary in Buffalo or Detroit, and but a pittance elsewhere. So persistent was the democratic trend that local government in much of the Old Northwest was placed in the hands of unpaid merchants and professional men during the post-frontier era, on the theory that they would remain closer to the people than politicians.

In the rural counties of the Old Northwest the story was the same. A case study of grass-roots democracy in Trempealeau County, Wisconsin, during its pioneer period, is revealing in this respect. There county affairs were entrusted to a board of supervisors; township affairs to an annual town meeting. Although both institutions were imported, with their authority and delineation of functions prescribed by the state legislature, their operations showed marked differences from their counterparts in the East. Popular participation in town meetings was unusually high, ranging between 62 percent and 73 percent of all adult males; these meetings were also notable for spirited debates that revealed a lively interest in democratic processes. This same interest produced an exceptionally large number of candidates for county and township offices, many of them young recent arrivals who felt themselves better able to represent the people than older leaders. Members of the status group in control were so seriously threatened by these upstarts that they had to choose between defeat and welcoming their challengers into party councils where they were allowed a minor share of patronage. These pressures kept politics in a constant state of flux, with frequent elections, abundant candidates, and an unusual opportunity for all to participate in political decision making. Here, in other words, was a community practicing a vigorous brand of democracy.

The result was not anarchy, for voters showed an instinctive preference for experienced candidates whose wealth was above the average. Trempealeau County during its pioneer period elevated thirty-two men to major political responsibility and 169 to minor posts. All were well-to-do, but some of the richest men were passed by, suggesting that wealth alone did not make a man a leader. Nearly all were American-born, most in the Northeastern states, although the number of foreign-born in minor leadership roles grew from 26 percent to 56 percent as the immigrant population of the county increased from 40 percent to 63 percent of the whole. During the earliest years, 83 percent of the leadership group were farmers, a figure that later fell to 67 percent as government functions were assumed by professional and businessmen. If Trempealeau County is typical of the West, pioneers chose political leaders who had some experience in the democratic United States, who were above the average in wealth, and who shared their own problems and beliefs; farmers seemed inclined to elect farmers as local officials, whatever their educational or military backgrounds. Most significant of all was the fact that in Trempealeau County twenty-six of the thirty-two major leaders assumed their roles in the first decade of the community, and only six in the next decade. Clearly in that fluid pioneer society the opportunity for political advancement—and hence the achievement of status—was greatest on the raw frontier and diminished with the thickening of population. Here again is a suggestion that pioneering did stimulate democratic tendencies.

This becomes increasingly apparent if we contrast Wisconsin with the South of that same day. There, even on the frontiers, an atypical process of settlement created a social setting quite different from that in Northern pioneer communities. In the better-soil regions of Alabama and Mississippi or of Arkansas and Texas large planters usually began arriving only two or three years after the first settlement, with money to buy up several farms for consolidation into a plantation. Their coming introduced an elite class accustomed to leadership and helped expel a poorer class of small farmers who would provide a bulwark for democracy. These planters, with the support of a community whose respect they expected and achieved, simply perpetuated the tested forms of local government they had known in the East. Undemocratic county courts, monopolizing all executive and legislative as well as judicial functions, became the typical governing units of the Old Southwest. Yet their authority did not go untested, for the democratic impulse was powerful enough to secure the election rather than appointment of a few county-court members in Alabama, and the separation of judicial and legislative functions on the local level.

The Southwest lagged behind the Northwest in democratic reform, but the frontier did loosen the bonds of custom even there.

Against this background of historical evidence, the question can now be asked: Did America's pioneering experience create or alter its democracy? In answering, one fact emerges at once. The West was not a breeding ground but a spawning ground for democratic theory and practice. Whether framing a constitution or drafting a town charter, frontiersmen were imitative rather than creative; they preferred to copy tested clauses from frames of government proved in the East to experimenting with more democratic new provisions. This was true even during the Populist period when the West flamed with dissent; the constitutions of the Omnibus States admitted in 1889 and 1890 were borrowed from those of older states no less than that of Ohio. Happily, however, the democracy so dear to the Westerner was universally popular at that time; manhood suffrage and devices extending popular control were demanded in the East as fervently as in the West. The abolition of property qualifications for voting inspired a crusade that swept Massachusetts and New York into line in the 1820's, and in the 1840's touched off a minor war in Rhode Island. When Westerners drafted their frames of government they had only to sort out the most suitable from the old, with many examples from which to choose. Thus, though imitative, they tended to copy the more democratic features of Eastern constitutions to create Western constitutions that were more democratic than their models. "The departures from long established usages," noted a Westerner, "have tended gradually, and almost uniformly, to democracy."

In still other ways the existence of a frontier served as a democratizing influence during the nineteenth century. As long as the nation believed that cheap lands would lure workmen westward, Eastern conservatives would be inclined to accept democratic reforms, for the liberalization of the franchise seemed a cheap price to pay for checking a migration that would deplete tax and labor rolls. The equality of opportunity usual on frontiers also played a role; in the West the rich became richer but the poor a good deal less poor and so more determined to share in the government to which they looked for future economic gains. Unusual opportunities for self-advancement in the West similarly released new talents and energies, many of which found expression in political activity, just as they would in any area undergoing change. Equally important was the fact that frontier mobility subjected imported institutions to heavy strains; every county that gained population demanded a greater voice in governmental affairs, and every one that failed to gain struggled to retain its power. This meant a wider range of discussion than in stabilized communities, and more frequent voting. The democratic processes were given an opportunity to operate more often on the frontiers, and strengthened accordingly.

The sum total of these changes was to vest greater control of the government in *all* the people, and to remove it from the hands of any elite, whether hereditary or economic. This seemed fair in a land where class lines were disappearing; who would dare deny a voice in governmental decision making to a humble newcomer who might make a fortune before nightfall or charm his fellow citizens into a place among the political elite at the next election? Men should not be treated as equals only because the Declaration of Independence *decreed* them equal, but because they could actually *be* equal amidst the opportunities of a new land. These democratic attitudes were not carried to the New World on the *Susan Constant* and the *Mayflower*. They were a product of the turbulent social scene created by the westering urge of the pioneers.

ALEXIS DE TOCQUEVILLE

The Inadequacy of Physical Causes

Alexis de Tocqueville, in Democracy in America, *speculates fruitfully on the factors that sustain democracy in the United States, and assesses the relative weights to be attributed to environment and inheritance.*

Accidental or Providential Causes Which Contribute to the Maintenance of the Democratic Republic in the United States

IT WOULD BE EASY for me to adduce a great number of secondary causes which have contributed to establish, and which concur to maintain, the democratic republic of the United States. But I discern two principal circumstances among these favourable ele-

From Alexis de Tocqueville, *Democracy in America,* I, 317–319, 348–350, 352, 359–360. New York: J. and H. G. Langley, 1841. Trans. by Henry Reeve.

ments, which I hasten to point out. I have already observed that the origin of the American settlements may be looked upon as the first and most efficacious cause, to which the present prosperity of the United States may be attributed. The Americans had the chances of birth in their favour; and their forefathers imported that equality of conditions into the country, whence the democratic republic has very naturally taken its rise. Nor was this all they did; for beside this republican condition of society, the early settlers bequeathed to their descendants those customs, manners, and opinions, which contribute most to the success of a republican form of government. When I reflect upon the consequences of this primary circumstance, methinks I see the destiny of America embodied in the first Puritan who landed on those shores, just as the human race was represented by the first man.

The chief circumstance which has favoured the establishment and the maintenance of a democratic republic in the United States, is the nature of the territory which the Americans inhabit. Their ancestors gave them the love of equality and of freedom: but God himself gave them the means of remaining equal and free, by placing them upon a boundless continent, which is open to their exertions. General prosperity is favourable to the stability of all governments, but more particularly of a democratic constitution, which depends upon the disposition of the majority, and more particularly of that portion of the community which is most exposed to feel the pressure of want. When the people rules, it must be rendered happy, or it will overturn the state: and misery is apt to stimulate it to those excesses to which ambition rouses kings. The physical causes, independent of the laws, which contribute to promote general prosperity, are more numerous in America than they have ever been in any other country in the world, at any other period of history. In the United States, not only is legislation democratic, but nature herself favours the cause of the people. . . .

Everything is extraordinary in America, the social condition of the inhabitants, as well as the laws; but the soil upon which these institutions are founded is more extraordinary than all the rest. When man was first placed upon the earth by the Creator, that earth was inexhaustible in its youth; but man was weak and ignorant: and when he had learned to explore the treasures which it contained, hosts of his fellow-creatures covered its surface, and he was obliged to earn an asylum for repose and for freedom by the sword. At that same period North America was discovered, as if it had been kept in reserve by the Deity, and had just risen from beneath the waters of the deluge.

*   *   *

The Laws Contribute More to the Maintenance of the Democratic Republic in the United States than the Physical Circumstances of the Country, and the Manners More than the Laws

I have remarked that the maintenance of democratic institutions in the United States is attributable to the circumstances, the laws, and the manners of that country.[1] Most Europeans are only acquainted with the first of these three causes, and they are apt to give it a preponderating importance which it does not really possess.

It is true that the Anglo-Americans settled in the New World in a state of social equality; the low-born and the noble were not to be found among them; and professional prejudices were always as entirely unknown as the prejudices of birth. Thus, as the condition of society was democratic, the empire of democracy was established without difficulty. But this circumstance is by no means peculiar to the United States; almost all the transatlantic colonies were founded by men equal among themselves, or who became so by inhabiting them. In no one part of the New World have Europeans been able to create an aristocracy. Nevertheless democratic institutions prosper nowhere but in the United States.

The American Union has no enemies to contend with; it stands in the wilds like an island in the ocean. But the Spaniards of South America were no less isolated by nature; yet their position has not relieved them from the charge of standing armies. They make war upon each other when they have no foreign enemies to oppose; and the Anglo-American democracy is the only one which has hitherto been able to maintain itself in peace.

The territory of the Union presents a boundless field to human activity, and inexhaustible materials for industry and labour. The passion of wealth takes the place of ambition, and the warmth of faction is mitigated by a sense of prosperity. But in what portion of the globe shall we meet with more fertile plains, with mightier rivers, or with more unexplored and inexhaustible riches, than in South America?

[1] I remind the reader of the general signification which I give to the word *manners*, namely, the moral and intellectual characteristics of social man taken collectively.

Nevertheless South America has been unable to maintain democratic institutions. If the welfare of nations depended on their being placed in a remote position, with an unbounded space of habitable territory before them, the Spaniards of South America would have no reason to complain of their fate. And although they might enjoy less prosperity than the inhabitants of the United States, their lot might still be such as to excite the envy of some nations in Europe. There are, however, no nations upon the face of the earth more miserable than those of South America.

Thus, not only are physical causes inadequate to produce results analogous to those which occur in North America, but they are unable to raise the population of South America above the level of European states, where they act in a contrary direction. Physical causes do not therefore affect the destiny of nations so much as has been supposed.

I have met with men in New England who were on the point of leaving a country, where they might have remained in easy circumstances, to go to seek their fortune in the wilds. Not far from that district I found a French population in Canada which was closely crowded on a narrow territory, although the same wilds were at hand; and while the emigrant from the United States purchased an extensive estate with the earnings of a short term of labour, the Canadian paid as much for land as he would have done in France. Nature offers the solitudes of the New World to Europeans; but they are not always acquainted with the means of turning her gifts to account. Other peoples of America have the same physical conditions of prosperity as the Anglo-Americans, but without their laws and their manners; and these peoples are wretched. The laws and manners of the Anglo-Americans are therefore that efficient cause of their greatness which is the object of my inquiry.

*   *   *

The manners of the Americans of the United States are . . . the real cause which renders that people the only one of the American nations that is able to support a democratic government; and it is the influence of manners which produces the different degrees of order and of prosperity, that may be distinguished in the several Anglo-American democracies. Thus the effect which the geographical position of a country may have upon the duration of democratic institutions is exaggerated in Europe. Too much importance is attributed to legislation, too little to manners. These three great causes serve, no doubt, to regulate and direct the American democracy; but if they were to be classed in their proper order, I should say that the physical circumstances are less efficient than the laws, and the laws very subordinate to the manners of the people. I am convinced that the most advantageous situation and the best possible laws cannot maintain a constitution in spite of the manners of a country: while the latter may turn the most unfavourable positions and the worst laws to some advantage. The importance of manners is a common truth to which study and experience incessantly direct our attention. It may be regarded as a central point in the range of human observation, and the common termination of all inquiry. So seriously do I insist upon this head, that if I have hitherto failed in making the reader feel the important influence which I attribute to the practical experience, the habits, the opinions, in short, to the manners of the Americans, upon the maintenance of their institutions, I have failed in the principal object of my work.

*   *   *

Importance of What Precedes with Respect to the State of Europe

Those who, after having read this book, should imagine that my intention in writing it has been to propose the laws and manners of the Anglo-Americans for the imitation of all democratic peoples, would commit a very great mistake; they must have paid more attention to the form than to the substance of my ideas. My aim has been to show, by the example of America, that laws, and especially manners, may exist, which will allow a democratic people to remain free. But I am very far from thinking that we ought to follow the example of the American democracy, and copy the means which it has employed to attain its ends; for I am well aware of the influence which the nature of a country and its political precedents exercise upon a constitution; and I should regard it as a great misfortune for mankind, if liberty were to exist, all over the world, under the same forms.

DAVID M. POTTER
Democracy and Abundance

David M. Potter, Professor of History at Stanford University, is author of Lincoln and His Party in the Secession Crisis *(1942) and* People of Plenty *(1954). In the following selection from the latter work Potter argues that the American political system is one of the "major by-products" of our material abundance and that it is workable "because of the measure of that abundance."*

BY VIEWING DEMOCRACY simply as a question of political morality, we have blinded ourselves to the fact that, in every country, the system of government is a by-product of the general conditions of life, including, of course, the economic conditions, and that democracy, like any other system, is appropriate for countries where these conditions are suited to it and inappropriate for others with unsuitable conditions, or at least that it is vastly more appropriate for some than for others. Viewed in these terms, there is a strong case for believing that democracy is clearly most appropriate for countries which enjoy an economic surplus and least appropriate for countries where there is an economic insufficiency. In short, economic abundance is conducive to political democracy.

At first glance this proposition may seem abjectly deterministic and may seem to imply that our democracy, like our climate, is a mere matter of luck, involving no merit. But it does not necessarily mean that we enjoy democracy without achieving it; rather, it means that we have achieved it less by sheer ideological devotion to the democratic principle than by the creation of economic conditions in which democracy will grow. In doing this, we have, of course, enjoyed the advantage of unequaled natural resources, but, as I have already sought to show, abundant physical endowments do not automatically or invariably produce an economic surplus for the area which possesses them. For instance, New

England, poorly endowed by nature, became, in the nineteenth century, one of the richest regions of the United States, while the Cotton South, richly endowed, committed itself to a slave-labor system, a one-crop system, and an economy restricted to producing raw materials, which, in the end, left it the poorest part of the nation.

These instances and many others indicate that man may, through cultural processes, use environment well or use it ill; he may make his political system one of the instruments for such use; he may apply democratic devices for the purpose of developing or distributing abundance, and then he may use abundance as a base for the broadening and consolidation of his democracy. Or, to put it another way, he may use an economic surplus for the purpose of furthering a democratic system which will, in turn, enable him to increase further his economic surplus.

But, though this view does not, in a deterministic sense, deny man credit for democratic accomplishments, it does argue that he should distinguish very carefully the things for which credit is claimed. A nation may properly be proud that it has developed the economic means which enable it to afford a full-fledged democracy or that it has utilized democratic practices to create the economic base on which a democracy can be further broadened. But it cannot, with any validity, attribute its democracy to sheer moral and ideological virtue. . . .

To understand why a democratic system depends upon an economic surplus, one has only to compare what a democracy offers to its citizens and what other regimes offer. All social systems, of course, seek to keep the bulk of their people contented, and all of them make promises of one kind or another in order to do this—some have promised a utopia in the indefinite future; others have offered, instead of real welfare, inexpensive distractions such as the bread and circuses of the Romans or the lotteries of modern Spain and Latin America; still others have attempted to provide real cradle-to-the-grave security. But however much or little a society, or a government acting for the society, may have to allot, it is axiomatic that it must not arouse expectations very much higher than it is able to satisfy. This means that it must not hold out the promise of opportunity unless there is a reasonable prospect of the opportunity's being fulfilled. It must not invite the individual to compete for prizes unless there are a substantial number of awards to be passed out.

In all societies of economic insufficiency, which is the only kind that existed up to about two centuries ago, certain social conditions have been fixed and inevitable. The vast majority of the people were inescapably destined to heavy toil and bare subsistence, and the economic surplus in excess of such bare subsistence was not sufficient to give leisure and abundance to more than a tiny minority. In these circumstances, certainly the society could not afford either the economic or the emotional costs of conducting a great social steeplechase for the purpose of selecting a handful of winners to occupy the few enviable positions. It was much sounder public policy to assign these positions by an arbitrary system of status and at the same time to assign to the great bulk of the people the burdens which most of them were destined to bear regardless of what regime was in power. Under a system of subordination transmitted by heredity, social competition, with its attendant loss of energy through friction, was avoided; the status-bound individual often gained a sense of contentment with his lot and even of dignity within his narrow sphere, and all that he sacrificed for this psychological advantage was a statistically negligible chance for advancement. Moreover, in a relatively static and relatively simple society such as that of Tudor or Stuart England, the problems of government were not very intricate, and the only qualities required in the local ruling class were integrity and a willingness to accept responsibility. These qualities could usually be found and could readily be transmitted even in a squirearchy of low intellectual attainments, and therefore there was no need to recruit widely for leadership, as a society must do when it requires intelligence, specialized skill, and adaptability in its administration.

A country with inadequate wealth, therefore, could not safely promise its citizens more than security of status—at a low level in the social hierarchy and with a meager living. But this promise is, in its denial of equality, by definition, undemocratic. A democracy, by contrast, setting equality as its goal, must promise opportunity, for the goal of equality becomes a mockery unless there is some means of attaining it. But in promising opportunity, the democracy is constantly arousing expectations which it lacks the current means to fulfil and is betting on its ability to procure the necessary means by the very act of stimulating people to demand them and go after them. It is constantly educating large numbers of people without waiting to see whether jobs requiring education are available for all of them; it does this in the expectation that the supply will create a demand and that a society constantly rising in the level of its education will constantly generate new posts in which educated people are needed. Also, democracy is forever encouraging individuals to determine their own goals and set their own courses toward these goals, even though only a small proportion can attain complete success; the time and effort of many may be wasted in the pursuit, but the advantage to society of having the maximum number of people developing their maximum potentialities of intellect and personality is thought to justify the social cost.

All this is very well and works admirably if the country following these practices has the necessary physical resources and human resourcefulness to raise the standard of living, to create new occupational opportunities, and to find outlets for the abilities of an ever increasing class of trained men. But it must have this endowment to begin with, or it is certain to suffer intensely from the social waste that results from giving training which cannot be utilized and from the psychological damage that results when a competition has an excess of participants and a paucity of rewards. In short, to succeed as a democracy, a country must enjoy an economic surplus to begin with or must contrive to attain one.

*   *   *

Not only has the presence of more than enough seats, more than enough rewards for those who strive, made the maintenance of a democratic system possible in America; it has also given a characteristic tone to American equalitarianism as distinguished from the equalitarianism of the Old World. Essentially, the difference is that Europe has always conceived of redistribution of wealth as necessitating the expropriation of some and the corresponding aggrandizement of others; but America has conceived of it primarily in terms of giving to some without taking from others. Hence, Europe cannot think of altering the relationship between the various levels of society without assuming a class struggle; but America has altered and can alter these relationships without necessarily treating one class as the victim or even, in an ultimate sense, the antagonist of another. The European mind often assumes implicitly that the volume of wealth is fixed; that most of the potential wealth has already been converted into actual wealth; that this actual wealth is already in the hands of owners; and, therefore, that the only way for one person or group to secure more is to wrest it from some other person or group, leaving that person or group with less. The British Labour party, for instance, has, I believe, placed greater emphasis upon the heavy taxation of the wealthy and less upon the increase of productive capacity than an American labor party might have done. The American mind, by contrast, often assumes implicitly that the volume of wealth is dynamic, that much potential wealth still remains to be converted; and that diverse groups—for instance, capital and labor—can take more wealth out of the environment by working together than they can take out of one another by class warfare.

European radical thought is prone to demand that the man of property be stripped of his carriage and his fine clothes; but American radical thought is likely to insist, instead, that the ordinary man is entitled to mass-produced copies, indistinguishable from the originals. Few Americans feel entirely at ease with the slogan "Soak the rich," but the phrase "Deal me in" springs spontaneously and joyously to American lips.

*   *   *

Occasionally, one encounters the statement that Americans believe in leveling up rather than in leveling down. The truth of the assertion is more or less self-evident, but the basic meaning is less so. Clearly, if one is leveling a fixed number of items, say, personal incomes, the very process of leveling implies the reduction of the higher ones. But in order to raise the lower without reducing the higher, to level *up*, it is necessary to increase the total of all the incomes—that is, to introduce new factors instead of solving the problem with the factors originally given. And it is by this stratagem of refusing to accept the factors given, of drawing on nature's surplus and on technology's tricks, that America has often dealt with her problems of social reform.

This, in turn, may explain another distinctive feature of the American record, and that is the relative lack of intellectualism in its reform or radical movements. For instance, by European standards the Populists of the late nineteenth century, and even more the Progressives of the early twentieth, would have seemed incredibly muddled, sentimental, and superficial in their thinking. European radicalism almost invariably has had a highly articulated rationale, a fully developed doctrinal system. European radicals have kept their ideological weapons sharpened to razor edge, so that they are ever ready to follow logic through the most complex maze or to split the hairs of heresy in disputes over minor points of doctrine. They do this, in part, I believe, because the social problems with which they deal are relatively fixed, and disciplined intelligence is the one means through which they can hope to attain a solution. But the social problems of America were not at all fixed, and their mutability has made logical solutions unnecessary.

Our practice, indeed, has been to overleap problems—to by-pass them—rather than to solve them. For instance, in the 1880's and 1890's there seemed to be three major public problems—the problem of a shrinking bullion supply; the problem of the control of an entire industry by a small group of monopolists, like John D. Rockefeller and his associates in the oil industry; and the problem of regulation of the railroads, which enjoyed a natural monopoly of transportation. Reformers struggled with all three of these problems, and various political solutions were proposed: the adoption of a bimetallic currency to relieve the bullion stringency, the enactment of an anti-trust law to curb Mr. Rockefeller, and the adoption of an Interstate Commerce Act to protect the shipper vis-à-vis the railroads. But in each case technological change interposed to relieve the acuteness of the problem or even to make it obsolete: the discovery of new gold supplies in the Klondike and of new methods of recovering gold reversed the process of shrinkage in the bullion supply; the discovery of the vast new deposits of oil in Texas and elsewhere undermined the dominance of Rockefeller in the oil industry as no legislative prohibition was ever able to do; and the introduction of trucks moving over a network of national highways ended the natural monopoly of transportation by the railroads before Congress ceased the long quest for a legislative solution.

*   *   *

Writers on public questions often assume that in our early history we had a basic commitment to individualism and that we have recently abandoned this traditional principle just for the sake of security. But what we really were committed to was realizing on the potentialities of our unmatched assets and raising our standard of living. Because the standard of living involves comfort and material things, a basic concern with it is commonly regarded as ignoble; yet, as I have already suggested, it is only because we have attained a relatively high standard of living that we can afford to own and operate a democratic system. But, whether noble or not, our commitment to abundance was primary, and individualism was sanctioned as the very best means of fulfilling the possibilities of abundance. When it ceased to be the best means, we modified it with a readiness alarming to people who had supposed that it was the individualism itself which was basic. We did this because a great many people had never regarded it, at bottom, as more than a means to an end. The politics of our democracy was a politics of abundance rather than a politics of individualism, a politics of increasing our wealth quickly rather than of dividing it precisely, a politics which smiled both on those who valued abundance as a means to safeguard freedom and on those who valued freedom as an aid in securing abundance.

In so far as Americans have succeeded in equating abundance and freedom, it becomes something of an abstraction to question which is the means and which is the end. The historical analyst may itch to discover which one is basic and which derivative, but the purpose of Americans, generally, will be to make the two coincide in such a way that, as factors, they cannot be isolated. In this sense it may seem somewhat metaphysical to make heavy-handed distinctions between these two ingredients—freedom and abundance—which are to such a great extent fused in American democratic thought.

But, though Americans have caused freedom and abundance to converge, the two are not by nature prone to convergence, and for the world at large they have not been closely linked. Consequently, when America, out of her abundance, preaches the gospel of democracy to countries which see no means of attaining abundance, the message does not carry the meaning which it is meant to convey. No other part of American activity has been so consistently and so completely a failure as our attempt to export democracy. At this point, the duality between abundance and freedom in the American democratic formula ceases to be abstract and becomes painfully concrete, for it is the lack of understanding of what we have to offer to the rest of the world that has vitiated our efforts to fulfil a national mission which we undertook with real dedication and for which we have made real sacrifices.

III Relevance or Uniqueness

SEYMOUR M. LIPSET

The First New Nation

Seymour M. Lipset is Professor of Social Relations and Government at Harvard University. Among his works are Agrarian Socialism *(1950);* with others, Union Democracy *(1956);* with R. Bendix, Social Mobility in Industrial Society *(1959);* Political Man *(1960); and, as editor,* The Elites in Latin America *(1967). In this selection reprinted from his* The First New Nation, *Lipset stresses the similarities between the position of Asia and Africa and that of the United States after it broke away from Great Britain.*

THE UNITED STATES may properly claim the title of the first new nation. It was the first major colony successfully to break away from colonial rule through revolance. It was, of course, followed within a few decades by most of the Spanish colonies in Central and South America. But while the United States exemplifies a new nation which successfully developed an industrial economy, a relatively integrated social structure (the race issue apart) and a stable democratic polity, most of the nations of Latin America do not. They remain underdeveloped economically, divided internally along racial, class, and (in some cases) linguistic lines, and have unstable polities, whether democratic or dictatorial. So perhaps the first new nation can contribute more than money to the latter-day ones; perhaps its development can give us some clues as to how revolutionary equalitarian and populist values may eventually become incorporated into a stable nonauthoritarian polity. . . .

There is a tendency for older nations to view with impatience the internal turmoil of new ones, and to become especially

From *The First New Nation,* pp. 15-16, 90-98. © 1963 by Seymour Martin Lipset, Basic Books, Inc., Publishers, New York.

alarmed at the way oligarchical-dictatorial and revolutionary forces shake their tenuous foundations. Coupled with this is a tendency to expect them to accomplish in a decade what other nations have taken a century or more to do. A backward glance into our own past should destroy the notion that the United States proceeded easily toward the establishment of democratic political institutions. In the period which saw the establishment of political legitimacy and party government, it was touch and go whether the complex balance of forces would swing in the direction of a one- or two-party system, or even whether the nation would survive as an entity. It took time to institutionalize values, beliefs, and practices, and there were many incidents that revealed how fragile the commitments to democracy and nationhood really were.

But it was from this crucible of confusion and conflict that values and goals became defined, issues carved out, positions taken, in short *an identity established*. For countries, like people, are not handed identities at birth, but acquire them through the arduous process of "growing up," a process which is a notoriously painful affair.

*   *   *

All states that have recently gained independence are faced with two interrelated problems, legitimating the use of political power and establishing national identity. And if it is a democratic polity they seek to establish, they must develop institutional and normative constraints upon efforts to inhibit organized opposition or to deny civil liberties to individual critics of those in power.

This section has explored ways in which these problems were confronted in the early history of the United States. National identity was formed under the aegis, first of a charismatic authority figure, and later under the leadership of a dominant "left wing" or revolutionary party led successively by three Founding Fathers. The pressures in new nations to outlaw opposition movements were reduced in America by the rapid decline of the conservative opposition. The revolutionary, democratic values that thus became part of the national self-image, and the basis for its authority structure, gained legitimacy as they proved effective— that is, as the nation prospered.

The need to establish stable authority and a sense of identity led the leaders of the United States to resist efforts by "old states" to involve the young nation in their quarrels. But at the same time that Americans rejected "foreign entanglements," they clearly used the Old World as both a negative and a positive point of reference, rejecting its political and class structures as backward, but nevertheless viewing its cultural and economic achievements as worthy of emulation. The intellectuals in particular expressed this ambivalence, since they played a major role in establishing and defining the state; but they then found that the task of operating and even living in it required them to conform to vulgar populist and provincial values.

In specifying those processes in the evolution of the first new nation that are comparable to what has been taking place in the societies of Asia and Africa in our own time, I am relying upon analogy. It ought to go without saying that: "We cannot assume that because conditions in one century led to certain effects, even roughly parallel conditions in another century would lead to similar effects. Neither can we be sure, of course, that the conditions were even roughly parallel." It is fairly obvious that conditions in the early United States were quite different from those faced by most of the new nations of today. Many of the internal conditions that hamper the evolution of stable authority and a unifying sense of national identity in the new nations of the twentieth century were much less acute in the early United States. But the evidence suggests that despite its advantages, the United States came very close to failing in its effort to establish a unified legitimate authority. The first attempt to do so in 1783, following on Independence, was a failure. The second and successful effort was endangered by frequent threats of secession and the open flaunting of central authority until the Civil War. The advantages which the early United States possessed, as compared with most of the contemporary new states, then, only show more strongly how significant the similarities are.

There were other American advantages that should be mentioned. Although internal conflicts stemming from attitudes toward the French Revolution disrupted the young American polity, there was no worldwide totalitarian conspiracy seeking to upset political and economic development from within, and holding up an alternative model of seemingly successful economic growth through the use of authoritarian methods. Also the absence of rapid mass communication systems meant that Americans were relatively isolated, and hence did not immediately compare their conditions with those in the more developed countries. The United States did not so urgently face a "revolution of rising expectations" based on the knowledge that life is much better elsewhere. The accepted concepts of natural or appropriate rights did not include a justification of the lower classes' organized participation in the polity to gain higher income, welfare support from the state, and the like. And whatever the exaggeration in the effects frequently attributed to the existence of an open land frontier, there can be little doubt that it contributed to social stability.

Internal value cleavages, which frustrate contemporary new nations, were comparatively less significant in young America. Shils points out that in today's new nations "the parochialism of kinship, caste and locality makes it difficult to create stable and coherent nation-wide parties." None of these parochialisms was as strong in the United States which was formed by a relatively homogeneous population with a common language, a relatively similar religious background (although denominational differences did cause some problems), and a common cultural and political tradition.

American social structure did not possess those great "gaps" which, in the contemporary new states, "conspire to separate the ordinary people from their government." The culture with which the educated identified contrasted less strongly with that of the uneducated. The ideology in the name of which America made its revolution was less alien to prevailing modes of thought than some of today's revolutionary creeds. Perhaps most important, the class structure of America, even before the establishment of the new nation, came closer to meeting the conditions for a stable democracy than do those of the new nations of our time—or, indeed, than those of the Old World at that time. Writing shortly before Independence was finally attained, Crèvecoeur, though sympathetic to the Tory cause, pointed up the egalitarianism of American society:

The rich and the poor are not so far removed from each other as they are in Europe. . . . A pleasing uniformity of decent competence appears throughout our habitations. . . . It must take some time ere he [the foreign traveler] can reconcile himself to our dictionary, which is but short in words of dignity, and names of honor. . . . Here man is as free as he ought to be; nor is this pleasing equality so transitory as many others are.

The ability to work the institutions of a democratic nation requires sophistication both at the elite level and the level of the citizenry at large. And as Carl Bridenbaugh has well demonstrated, the America of revolutionary times was not a colonial backwater. Philadelphia was the second largest English city—only London surpassed it in numbers. Philadelphia and other colonial American capitals were centers of relatively high culture at this time: they had universities and learned societies, and their elite was in touch with, and contributed to, the intellectual and scientific life of Britain.

In this respect, the political traditions that the American colonists held in common, were of particular importance since they included the concept of the rule of law, and even of constitutionalism. Each colony operated under a charter which defined and limited governmental powers. Although colonial subjects, Americans were also Englishmen and were thus accustomed to the rights and privileges of Englishmen. Through their local governments they actually possessed more rights than did most of the residents of Britain itself. In a sense, even before independence, Americans met a basic condition for democratic government, the ability to operate its fundamental institutions. . . .

In many contemporary new nations, a potentially politically powerful military class, who have a patriotic, national outlook, may use the army to seize power if it becomes impatient with civilian leadership. When the United States was seeking to establish a national authority, it was not bedeviled by such a class. The entire army in 1789 consisted of 672 men; and even after a decade of threats of war, there were only 3,429 soldiers in 1800. The potential military strength was, of course, much larger, for it included various state militia reserves. The latter, however, were simply the citizenry, and as long as the government had the loyalty of the general population, it had no need to fear its professional soldiers.

Of great significance in facilitating America's development as a nation, both politically and economically, was the fact that the weight of ancient tradition which is present in almost all of the contemporary new states was largely absent. It was not only a new nation, it was a new society, much less bound to the customs and values of the past than any nation of Europe. Crèvecoeur well described the American as a "new man," the likes of which had never been seen before.

Religion, of course, may be viewed as a "traditional" institution which played an important role in the United States. But in the first half-decade of the American Republic, as we have seen, the defenders of religious traditionalism were seriously weakened, as the various state churches—Anglican in the South and Congregationalist in New England—were gradually disestablished. Moreover, the new United States was particularly fortunate in the religious traditions which it did inherit. Calvinistic Puritanism, which was stronger in the colonies than in the mother country, was not as "uncongenial to modernity" as are some of the traditional beliefs inherited by new nations today. A positive orientation toward savings and hard work, and the strong motivation to achieve high positions that derives from this religious tradition, have been seen as causes of the remarkable economic expansion that made possible the legitimation of equalitarian values and democratic government. Max Weber, the most prominent exponent of the thesis that ascetic Protestantism played a major role in the development of capitalism in the Western world, argued that "one must never overlook that without the universal diffusion of these qualities and principles of a methodical way of life, qualities which were maintained through these [Calvinist] religious communities, capitalism, today, even in America, would not be what it is. . . ." Calvinism's "insistence that one's works were signs of eternal grace or damnation" has been transformed into a secular emphasis upon achievement.

Other Puritan influences on American development have perhaps not been sufficiently emphasized. As Richard Schlatter has pointed out in a recent summary of the researches on this subject, the Puritan tradition involved a respect for learning which led to the establishment of schools and universities on a scale that surpassed England. The opportunities for learning thus created, and the pressures for widespread education that equalitarian values implied, led to a wide distribution of literacy. The census of 1840 reported only 9 per cent of the white population twenty years old and over as illiterate.

The Puritan tradition may also have made it easier to legitimize American democracy as the rule of law. Tocqueville saw the special need of an egalitarian and democratic society for a self-restraining value system that would inhibit the tyranny of the majority, a function supposedly once fulfilled in the European societies by a secure and sophisticated aristocratic elite. In a democracy only religion could play this role, and therefore the less coercive the political institutions of such a society, the more it has need for a system of common belief to help restrict the actions of the rulers and the electorate. As he put it:

> But the revolutionists of America are obliged to profess an ostensible respect for Christian morality and equity, which does not permit them to violate wantonly the laws that oppose their designs; nor would they find it easy to surmount the scruples of their partisans even if they were able to get over their own. . . . Thus while the law permits Americans to do what they please, religion prevents them from conceiving, and forbids them to commit, what is rash or unjust.

While Tocqueville pointed out that Catholicism was not necessarily incompatible with democratic or egalitarian values, since "it confounds all the distinctions of society at the foot of the same altar," he describes the "form of Christianity" in early America as "a democratic and republican religion." It would indeed seem that the Calvinistic-Puritan tradition was particularly valuable in training men to the sort of self-restraint that Tocqueville felt was necessary for democracy. By making every man God's agent, ascetic Protestantism made each individual responsible for the state of morality in the society; and by making the congregation a disciplinary agent it helped to prevent any one individual from assuming that his brand of morality was better than others.

Puritanism had been associated with the movement of the squirearchy for political recognition in England. . . . So that, as Schlatter has pointed out, the Puritan tradition implied a concern for "constitutionalism and limited government," as well as a belief "that they are a peculiar people, destined by Providence to live in a more perfect community than any known in the Old World." . . .

In establishing its identity, the new America quickly came to see itself, and to be perceived by others, as a radical society in which conservatism and traditionalism had no proper place. The religious traditions on which it drew stressed that it was to be different from European nations. But its really radical character derived from its revolutionary origins. . . .

From Tocqueville and Martineau in the 1830's to Gunnar Myrdal in more recent times, foreign visitors have been impressed by the extent to which the values proclaimed in the Declaration of Independence have operated to prescribe social and political behavior. And the legitimacy which the American authority structure ultimately attained has been based on the assumption that as a nation it is dedicated to equality and to liberty, to the fulfillment of its original political objectives.

As Frank Thistlethwaite put it a few years ago:

In the mid-twentieth century the American people still pursue their Revolutionary ideal: A Republic established in the belief that men of good will could voluntarily come together in the sanctuary of an American wilderness to order their common affairs according to rational principles; a dedicated association in which men participate not by virtue of being born into it as heirs of immemorial custom, but by virtue of free choice, of the will to affirm certain sacred principles; a community of the uprooted, of migrants who have turned their back on the past in which they were born; . . . a society fluid and experimental, uncommitted to rigid values, cherishing freedom of will and choice and bestowing all the promise of the future on those with the manhood to reject the past.

SAMUEL P. HUNTINGTON

New Society, Old State

Samuel P. Huntington is Professor of Government and Chairman of the Department of Government at Harvard University. Among his books are The Soldier and the State *(1957);* The Common Defense *(1961); and, as coauthor,* Political Power: USA-USSR *(1964). His most recent research reflects his interest in the problems of political modernization. In the following selection his method, like Lipset's, is comparative, but he concludes that the disparities between the experience of the new countries of today and that of the United States as a young republic are far more significant than the similarities.*

From Samuel P. Huntington, "Political Modernization: America vs. Europe," *World Politics,* XVIII (April, 1966), 379–382, 401–414. Reprinted by permission of *World Politics.*

THREE DISTINCT PATTERNS of political modernization can be distinguished: Continental, British, and American. On the Continent the rationalization of authority and the differentiation of structures were dominant trends of the seventeenth century. . . . The modern state replaced the feudal principality; loyalty to the state superseded loyalty to church and to dynasty. . . . With the birth of the modern state came the subordination of the church, the suppression of the medieval estates, and the weakening of the aristocracy by the rise of new groups. In addition, the century witnessed the rapid growth and rationalization of state bureaucracies and public services, the origin and expansion of standing armies, and the extension and improvement of taxation. In 1600 the medieval political world was still a reality on the Continent; by 1700 it had been replaced by the modern world of nation-states.

The British pattern of evolution was similar in nature to that on the Continent but rather different in results. In Britain, too, church was subordinated to state, authority was centralized, sovereignty asserted internally as well as externally, legal and political institutions differentiated, bureaucracies expanded, and a standing army created. The efforts of the Stuarts, however, to rationalize authority along the lines of continental absolutism provoked a constitutional struggle, from which Parliament eventually emerged the victor. In Britain, as on the Continent, authority was centralized but it was centralized in Parliament rather than in the Crown. This was no less of a revolution than occurred on the Continent and perhaps even more of one.

In America, on the other hand, the political system did not undergo any revolutionary changes at all. Instead, the principal elements of the English sixteenth-century constitution were exported to the New World, took root there, and were given new life at precisely the time they were being abandoned in the home country. These Tudor institutions were still partially medieval in character. The Tudor century saw some steps toward modernization in English politics, particularly the establishment of the supremacy of the state over the church, a heightened sense of national identity and consciousness, and a significant increase in the power of the Crown and the executive establishment. . . . The changes introduced by the Tudor monarchs did not have "the effect of breaking down the essential principles of the medieval Constitution, nor even its structure." Among these principles and structures were the idea of the organic union of society and government, the harmony of authorities within government, the subordination of government to fundamental law, the intermingling of the legal and political realms, the balance of power between Crown and Parliament, the complementary representative roles of these two institutions, the vitality of local governmental authorities, and reliance on local forces for the defense of the realm.

The English colonists took these late medieval and Tudor political ideas, practices, and institutions across the Atlantic with them during the great migrations in the first half of the seventeenth century. The patterns of thought and behavior established in the New World developed and grew but did not substantially change during the century and a half of colonihood. . . . The conflict between the colonists and the British government in the middle of the eighteenth century served only to reinforce the colonists' adherence to their traditional patterns. . . . In the constitutional debates before the American Revolution, the colonists in effect argued the case of the old English constitution against the merits of the new British constitution which had come into existence during the century after they had left the mother country. "Their theory," as Pollard says, "was essentially medieval."

These ancient practices and ideas were embodied in the state constitutions drafted after independence and in the Federal Constitution of 1787. Not only is the American Constitution the oldest written national constitution in the world, but it is also a constitution which in large part simply codified and formalized on the national level practices and institutions that had long existed on the colonial level. The institutional framework established in 1787 has, in turn, changed remarkably little in 175 years. . . . The American political system of the twentieth century still bears a closer approximation to the Tudor polity of the sixteenth century than does the British political system of the twentieth century. . . . The British broke their traditional political patterns in the seventeenth century. The Americans did not do so then and have only partially done so since then. Political modernization in America has thus been strangely attenuated and incomplete. In institutional terms, the American polity has never been underdeveloped, but it has also never been wholly modern. In an age of rationalized authority, functional specialization, mass democracy, and totalitarian dictatorship, the American political system remains a curious anachronism. In today's world, the American political system is unique, if only because it is so antique.

*   *   *

The rationalization of authority and the differentiation of structure were slower and less complete in America than they were in Europe. Such was not the case with the third aspect of political modernization: the broadening of political participation. Here, if anything, America led Europe, although the differences in timing in the expansion of participation were less significant than the differences in the way in which that expansion took place. These contrasts in political evolution were directly related to the prevalence of foreign war and social conflict in Europe as contrasted with America.

On the Continent, the late sixteenth and the seventeenth centuries were periods of intense struggle and conflict. For only three years during the entire seventeenth century was there a complete absence of fighting on the European Continent. Several of the larger states were more often at war during the century than they were at peace. The wars were usually complex affairs involving many states tied together in dynastic and political alliances. War reached an intensity in the seventeenth century which it had never reached previously and which was exceeded later only in the twentieth century. The prevalence of war directly promoted political modernization. Competition forced the monarchs to build their military strength. The creation of military strength required national unity, the suppression of regional and religious dissidents, the expansion of armies and bureaucracies, and a major increase in state revenues. . . .

Largely because of its insular position, Great Britain was a partial exception to this pattern of war and insecurity. Even so, one major impetus to the centralization of authority in English government came from the efforts of the Stuart kings to collect more taxes to build and man more ships to compete with the French and other continental powers. If it were not for the English Channel, the Stuart centralization probably would have succeeded. In America in the seventeenth century, however, continuing threats came only from the Indians. The nature of this threat, plus the dispersion of the settlements, meant that the principal defense force had to be the settlers themselves organized into militia units. There was little incentive to develop European-type military forces and a European-type state to support and control them.

Civil harmony also contributed significantly to the preservation of Tudor political institutions in America. Those institutions reflected the relative unity and harmony of English society during the sixteenth century. English society, which had been racked by the Wars of the Roses in the fifteenth century, welcomed the opportunity for civil peace that the Tudors afforded. Social conflict was minor during the sixteenth century. The aristocracy had been almost eliminated during the civil wars of the previous century. England was not perhaps a middle-class society but the differences between social classes were less then than they had been earlier and much less than they were to become later. Individual mobility rather than class struggle was the keynote of the Tudor years. "The England of the Tudors was an 'organic state' to a degree unknown before Tudor times, and forgotten almost immediately afterward." Harmony and unity made it unnecessary to fix sovereignty in any particular institution; it could remain dispersed so long as social conflict was minimal.

The only major issue that disrupted the Tudor consensus was, of course, religion. Significantly, in sixteenth-century English history the Act of Supremacy meant the supremacy of the state over the church, not the supremacy of one governmental institution over another or one class over another. After the brief interlude of the Marian struggles, however, the shrewd politicking and popular appeal of Elizabeth restored a peace among religious groups which was virtually unique in Europe at that time. The balance between Crown and Parliament and the combination of an active monarchy and common law depended upon this social harmony. Meanwhile on the Continent, civil strife had already reached a new intensity before the end of the sixteenth century. France alone had eight civil wars during the thirty-six years between 1562 and 1598, a period roughly comprising the peaceful reign of Elizabeth in England. The following fifty years saw Richelieu's struggles with the Huguenots and the wars of the Fronde. Spain was racked by civil strife, particularly between 1640 and 1652 when Philip IV and Olivares attempted to subdue Catalonia. In Germany, princes and parliaments fought each other. Where, as frequently happened, estates and princes espoused different religions, the controversy over religion inevitably broke the medieval balance of powers between princes and parliaments.

English harmony ended with the sixteenth century. Whether the gentry were rising, falling, or doing both in seventeenth-century England, forces were at work in society disrupting Tudor social peace. The efforts to reestablish something like the Tudor balance broke down before the intensity of social and religious conflict. The brief period of Crown power between 1630 and 1640, for instance, gave way "to a short-lived restoration of something like the Tudor balance of powers during the first year of the Long Parliament (1641). This balance might perhaps have been sustained indefinitely but for the rise of acute religious differences between the Crown and the militant Puritan party in the Commons." In England, as in France, civil strife led to the demand for strong centralized power to reestablish public order. The breakdown of unity in society gave rise to irresistible forces to reestablish that unity through government.

Both Puritan and Cavalier emigrants to America escaped from English civil strife. The process of fragmentation, in turn, encouraged homogeneity, and homogeneity encouraged "a kind of immobility." In America, environment reinforced heredity, as the common challenges of the frontier combined with the abundance of land to help perpetuate the egalitarian characteristics of Tudor society and the complexity of Tudor political institutions. And paradoxically, as Hartz has pointed out, the framers of the Constitution of 1787 reproduced these institutions on the federal level in the belief that the social divisions and conflict within American society made necessary a complex system of checks and balances. In reality, however, their Constitution was successful only because their view of American society was erroneous. So also, only the absence of significant social divisions permitted the continued transformation of political issues into legal ones through the peculiar institution of judicial review. Divided societies cannot exist without centralized power; consensual societies cannot exist with it.

In continental Europe, as in most contemporary modernizing countries, rationalized authority and centralized power were necessary not only for unity but also for progress. The opposition to modernization came from traditional interests: religious, aristocratic, regional, and local. The centralization of power was necessary to smash the old order, break down the privileges and restraints of feudalism, and free the way for the rise of new social groups and the development of new economic activities. In some degree a coincidence of interest did exist between the absolute monarchs and the rising middle classes. Hence European liberals often viewed favorably the concentration of authority in an absolute monarch, just as modernizers today frequently view favorably the concentration of authority in a single "mass" party.

In America, on the other hand, the absence of feudal social institutions made the centralization of power unnecessary. Since there was no aristocracy to dislodge, there was no need to call into existence a governmental power capable of dislodging it. This great European impetus to political modernization was missing. Society could develop and change without having to overcome the opposition of social classes with a vested interest in the social and economic status quo. The combination of an egalitarian social inheritance plus the plenitude of land and other resources enabled social and economic development to take place more or less spontaneously. Government often helped to promote economic development, but (apart from the abolition of slavery) it played only a minor role in changing social customs and social structure. In modernizing societies, the centralization of power varies directly with the resistance to social change. In the United States, where the resistance was little, so also was the centralization.

The differences in social consensus between Europe and America also account for the differences in the manner in which political participation expanded. In Europe this expansion was marked by discontinuities on two levels. On the institutional level, democratization meant the shift of power from monarchical ruler to popular assembly. This shift began in England in the seventeenth century, in France in the eighteenth century, and in Germany in the nineteenth century. On the electoral level, democratization meant the extension of the suffrage for this assembly from aristocracy to upper bourgeoisie, lower bourgeoisie, peasants, and urban workers. The process is clearly seen in the English reform acts of 1832, 1867, 1884, and 1918. In America, on the other hand, no such class differences existed as in England. Suffrage was already widespread in most colonies by independence, and universal white manhood suffrage was a fact in most states by 1830. The unity of society and the division of government meant that the latter was the principal focus of democratization. The American equivalent of the Reform Act of 1832 was the change in the nature of the Electoral College produced by the rise of political parties, and the resulting transformation of the Presidency from an indirectly elected, semi-oligarchical office to a popular one. The other major steps in the expansion of popular participation in the United States involved the extension of the electoral principle to all the state governors, to both houses of the state legislatures, to many state administrative offices and boards, to the judiciary in many states, and to the United States Senate. Thus, in Europe the broadening of participation meant the extension of the suffrage for one institution to all classes of society, while in America it meant the extension of the suffrage by the one class in society to all (or almost all) institutions of government.

In Europe the opposition to modernization within society forced the modernization of the political system. In America, the ease of modernization within society precluded the modernization of the political system. The United States thus combines the world's most modern society with one of the world's most antique polities. The American political experience is distinguished by frequent acts of creation but few, if any, of innovation. Since the Revolution, constitutions have been drafted for thirty-eight new political systems, but the same pattern of government has been repeated over and over again. The new constitutions of Alaska and Hawaii differ only in detail from the constitution of Massachusetts, originally drafted by John Adams in 1780. When else in history has such a unique series of opportunities for political experiment and innovation been so almost totally wasted?

This static quality of the political system contrasts with the prevalence of change elsewhere in American society. A distinguishing feature of American culture, Robin Williams has argued, is its positive orientation toward change. In a similar vein, two observers have noted, "In the United States change itself is valued. The new is good; the old is unsatisfactory. Americans gain prestige by being among the first to own next year's automobile; in England, much effort is devoted to keeping twenty-five-year-old cars in operating condition." In three centuries, a few pitifully small and poor rural settlements strung along the Atlantic seaboard and populated in large part by religious exiles were transformed into a huge, urbanized, continental republic, the world's leading economic and military power. America has given the world its most modern and efficient economic organizations. It has pioneered social benefits for the masses: mass production, mass education, mass culture. Economically and socially, everything has been movement and change. Politically, however, the only significant institutional innovation has been federalism, and this, in itself, of course, was made possible only by the traditional hostility to the centralization of authority. Fundamental social and economic change has been combined with political stability and continuity. In a society dedicated to what is shiny new, the polity remains quaintly old.

Modernity is thus not all of a piece. The American experience demonstrates conclusively that some institutions and some aspects of a society may become highly modern while other institutions and other aspects retain much of their traditional form and substance. Indeed, this may be a natural state of affairs. In any system some sort of equilibrium or balance must be maintained between change and continuity. Change in some spheres renders unnecessary or impossible change in others. In America the continuity and stability of government has permitted the rapid change of society, and the rapid change in society has encouraged continuity and stability in government. The relation between polity and society may well be dialectical rather than complementary. In other societies, such as Latin America, a rigid social structure and the absence of social and economic change have been combined with political instability and the weakness of political institutions. A good case can be made, moreover, that the latter is the result of the former.

This combination of modern society and Tudor polity explains much that is otherwise perplexing about political ideas in America. In Europe the conservative is the defender of traditional institutions and values, particularly those in society rather than in government. Conservatism is associated with the church, the aristocracy, social customs, the established social order. The attitude of conservatives toward government is ambivalent: Government is viewed as the guarantor of social order, but it also is viewed as the generator of social change. Society rather than government has been the principal conservative concern. European liberals, on the other hand, have had a much more positive attitude toward government. Like Turgot, Price, and Godwin, they have viewed the centralization of power as the precondition of social reform. They have supported the gathering of power into a single place . . . where it can then be used to change society.

In America, on the other hand, these liberal and conservative attitudes have been thoroughly confused and partly reversed. Conservatism has seldom flourished because it has lacked social institutions to conserve. Society is changing and modern, while government, which the conservative views with suspicion, has been relatively unchanging and antique. With a few exceptions, such as a handful of colleges and churches, the oldest institutions in American society are governmental institutions. The absence of established social institutions, in turn, has made it unnecessary for American liberals to espouse the centralization of power as did

European liberals. John Adams could combine Montesquieu's polity with Turgot's society much to the bafflement of Turgot. Nineteenth-century Europeans had every reason to be fascinated by America: It united a liberal society which they were yet to experience with a conservative politics which they had in large part forgotten.

Recently much has been made of the relevance to the currently modernizing countries of Asia, Africa, and Latin America of the earlier phases of modernization in the United States. It has been argued that the United States was and still should be a revolutionary power. The American Revolution, it has been said, "started a chain reaction" beginning with the French Revolution and leading on to the Russian Revolution which was "the American Revolution's child, though an unwanted and unacknowledged one." But the effort to see connections and/or parallels between what happened in America in the eighteenth century and what is happening in Asia, Africa, and elsewhere in the twentieth century can only contribute to monstrous misunderstandings of both historical experiences. The American Revolution was not a social revolution like the French, Russian, Chinese, Mexican, or Cuban revolutions; it was a war of independence. Moreover, it was not a war of independence of natives against alien conquerors, like the struggles of the Indonesians against the Dutch, or of the Vietnamese or the Algerians against the French, but was instead a war of settlers against the home country. Any recent parallels are in the relation of the Algerian *colons* to the French Republic or of the Southern Rhodesians to the United Kingdom. It is in these cases, in the last of the European "fragments" to break their European ties, that the eighteenth-century experience of America may be duplicated. These, however, are not parallels of which American liberal intellectuals and statesmen like to be reminded.

The case for the relevance of the American experience to the contemporary modernizing countries has also been couched in terms of the United States as "The First New Nation." The United States, it has been argued, was the first nation "of any consequence to emerge from the colonial dominance of Western Europe as a sovereign state in its own right, and to that extent it shares something in common with the 'emerging nations' of today, no matter how different they may be in other respects." The phrase "new nation," however, fails to distinguish between state and society, and hence misses crucial differences between the American experience and those of the contemporary modernizing countries. The latter are, for the most part, more accurately described by the title of another book: "Old Societies and New States." America, on the other hand, was historically a new society but an old state. Hence the problems of government and political modernization that the contemporary modernizing states face differ fundamentally from those that confronted the United States.

In most countries of Asia, Africa, and Latin America, modernization faces tremendous social obstacles. The gaps between rich and poor, between modern elite and traditional mass, between the powerful and the weak—gaps that are the common lot of "old societies" trying to modernize today—contrast markedly with the "pleasing uniformity" of the "one estate" that existed in eighteenth-century America. As in seventeenth-century Europe these gaps can be overcome only by the creation of powerful, centralized authority in government. The United States never had to construct such authority in order to modernize its society, and hence its experience has little to offer modernizing countries today. America, De Tocqueville said, "arrived at a state of democracy without having to endure a democratic revolution" and "was born equal without having to become so." So also American society was born modern; and it hence was never necessary to construct a government powerful enough to make it so. An antique polity is compatible with a modern society but it is not compatible with the modernization of a traditional society.

The Latin American experience, for instance, is almost exactly the reverse of that of the United States. After independence the United States continued essentially the same political institutions it had had before independence, which were perfectly suited to its society. At independence the Latin American countries inherited and maintained an essentially feudal social structure. They attempted to superimpose on this social structure republican political institutions copied from the United States and revolutionary France. Such institutions had no meaning in a feudal society. These early efforts at republicanism left Latin America with weak governments which until the twentieth century lacked the authority and power to modernize the society. Liberal, pluralistic, democratic governments serve to perpetuate antiquated social structure. Thus in Latin America an inherent conflict exists between the political goals of the United States—elections, democracy, representative

government, pluralism, constitutionalism—and its social goals—
modernization, reform, social welfare, more equitable distribution
of wealth, development of a middle class. In the North American
experience these goals did not conflict. In Latin America, they
often clash head on. The variations of the North American political system which North Americans would like to reproduce in
Latin America are simply too weak, too diffuse, too dispersed to
mobilize the political power necessary to bring about fundamental
change. Such power can be mobilized by revolution, as it was in
Mexico and Cuba, and a historical function of revolutions is to
replace weak governments by strong governments capable of
achieving social change. The question for Latin America and similarly situated countries is whether other ways short of violent
revolution exist for generating the political power necessary to
modernize traditional societies.

However it occurs, the accumulation of power necessary for modernization makes the future of democracy rather bleak. Countries,
such as France and Prussia, which took the lead in political modernization in the seventeenth century have had difficulty in maintain-
ing stable democracy in the twentieth century. Countries in which
the seventeenth-century tendencies toward absolute monarchy
were either defeated (England), stalemated (Sweden), or absent
(America) later tended to develop more viable democratic institutions. The continued vitality of medieval estates and pluralistic
assemblies is associated with subsequent democratic tendencies. . . .

If a parallel exists between seventeenth-century modernization
and twentieth-century modernization, the implications of the
former for the latter are clear. Despite arguments to the contrary,
the countries where modernization requires the concentration of
power in a single, monolithic, hierarchical, but "mass," party are
not likely to be breeding grounds for democracy. Mass participation goes hand-in-hand with authoritarian control. As in Guinea
and Ghana, it is the twentieth-century weapon of modernizing
centralizers against traditional pluralism. Democracy, on the other
hand, is more likely in those countries that preserve elements of
traditional social and political pluralism. Its prospects are brightest
where traditional pluralism is adapted to modern politics, as appears to be the case with the caste associations of India and as
may be the case with tribal associations in some parts of Africa.
So also, Lebanon, the most democratic Arab country—indeed, perhaps the only democratic Arab country—has a highly traditional

politics of confessional pluralism. Like the states of seventeenth-century Europe, the non-Western countries of today can have political modernization or they can have democratic pluralism, but they cannot normally have both.

In each historical period one type of political system usually seems to its contemporaries to be particularly relevant to the needs and demands of the age. In the era of European state-building in the seventeenth century, the "pattern-state," to use Sir George Clark's phrase, was the Bourbon monarchy of France. Indeed, the new state that emerged in that century, as Clark argues, "may be called the French type of monarchy not only because it reached its strongest and most logical expression in France, but also because it was consciously and deliberately copied elsewhere from the Bourbon model." This type of centralized, absolute monarchy met the paramount needs of the time. In the late eighteenth and nineteenth centuries, the pattern-state was the British parliamentary system. The countries of Europe then faced the problems of democratization and the incorporation into the polity of the lower social orders. The British system furnished the model for this phase of modernization. Today, in much of Asia, Africa, and Latin America, political systems face simultaneously the needs to centralize authority, to differentiate structure, and to broaden participation. The system that seems most relevant to the simultaneous achievement of these goals is a one-party system. If Versailles set the standard for one century and Westminster for another, the Kremlin may well be the most relevant model for the modernizing countries of this century. The heads of minor German principalities aped Louis XIV; the heads of equally small and backward states today may ape Lenin and Mao. The primary need their countries face is the accumulation and concentration of power, not its dispersion, and it is in Moscow and Peking and not in Washington that this lesson is to be learned.

Nor should this irrelevance of the American polity come as a great surprise. Historically foreigners have always found American society more attractive than the American polity. Even in the seventeenth and eighteenth centuries, as Beloff observes, "the political appeal of the new country was less potent than the social one." De Tocqueville was far more impressed by the democracy of American society and customs than he was by its democratic institutions of government. In the last century Europeans have found much to emulate in American business organization and in American culture, but they have found little reason to copy American political institutions. Parliamentary democracies and one-party dictatorships abound throughout the world. But surely one of the striking features of world politics is the rarity of other political systems based on the American presidential model.

The irrelevance of the American polity to the rest of the world, however, must not be overdone. It is of little use to societies that must modernize a traditional order. But, as the American experience itself demonstrates, a Tudor polity is quite compatible with a modern society. Consequently it is possible, although far from necessary, that as other societies become more fully modern, as the need to disestablish old, traditional, feudal, and local elements declines, the need to maintain a political system capable of modernization may also disappear. Such a system will, of course, have the advantage of tradition and of association with successful social change, so the probabilities are that it will not change greatly. But at least the possibility exists that there may be some evolution toward an American-type system. The "end of ideology" in Western Europe, the mitigation of class conflict, the tendencies toward an "organic society," all suggest that the European countries could now tolerate more dispersed and relaxed political institutions. Some elements of the American system seem to be creeping back into Europe from which they were exported three centuries ago. Judicial review has made a partial and timorous reappearance on the Continent. After De Gaulle, the constitution of the Fifth Republic might well shake down to something not too far removed from the constitution of the American Republic. Mr. Harold Wilson was accused, before and after coming to power, of acting like Mr. President. These are small straws in the wind. They may not mean anything. But if they do mean anything, they mean that the New Europe may eventually come to share some of the old institutions that the New World has preserved from an older Europe.

IV Pluralistic Diversity or Elite Dominance

JOHN FISCHER

Neo-Calhounism

John Fischer, after fourteen years as editor-in-chief of Harper's
Magazine, *relinquished the post in July, 1967 and became a
contributing editor; he has written most of the magazine's
"Easy Chair" columns since 1955. Among his books are* Why
They Behave like Russians *(1947) and* The Stupidity Problem and Other Harassments *(1964). This selection is from an
article which argues that the idea of the "concurrent majority,"
for which Calhoun contended in the pre-Civil War era, actually
became the working principle of American politics. Restated
in its modern form, Calhoun's pluralism means that essentially
every group in the nation has a veto on policies directly affecting it.*

CALHOUN SUMMED UP his political thought in what he called the
Doctrine of the Concurrent Majority. He saw the United States as
a nation of tremendous and frightening diversity—a collection of
many different climates, races, cultures, religions, and economic
patterns. He saw the constant tension among all these special
interests, and he realized that the central problem of American
politics was to find some way of holding these conflicting groups
together.

It could not be done by force; no one group was strong enough
to impose its will on all the others. The goal could be achieved
only by compromise—and no real compromise could be possible

if any threat of coercion lurked behind the door. Therefore, Calhoun reasoned, every vital decision in American life would have to be adopted by a "concurrent majority"—by which he meant, in effect, a unanimous agreement of all interested parties. No decision which affected the interests of the slaveholders, he argued, should be taken without their consent; and by implication he would have given a similar veto to every other special interest, whether it be labor, management, the Catholic church, old-age pensioners, the silver miners, or the corn-growers of the Middle West.

Under the goad of the slavery issue, Calhoun was driven to state his doctrine in an extreme and unworkable form. If every sectional interest had been given the explicit, legal veto power which he called for, the government obviously would have been paralyzed. (That, in fact, is precisely what seems to be happening today in the United Nations.) It is the very essence of the idea of "concurrent majority" that it cannot be made legal and official. It can operate effectively only as an informal, highly elastic, and generally accepted understanding. Perhaps the best example is the Quaker church meeting, where decisions are not reached by formal vote at all, but rather by a give-and-take discussion which continues until "the sense of the meeting" jells and is accepted by everybody present.

Moreover, government by concurrent majority can exist only when no one power is strong enough to dominate completely, *and then only when all of the contending interest groups recognize and abide by certain rules of the game.*

These rules are the fundamental bond of unity in American political life. They can be summed up as a habit of extraordinary toleration, plus "equality" in the peculiar American meaning of that term which cannot be translated into any other language, even into the English of Great Britain. Under these rules every group tacitly binds itself to tolerate the interests and opinions of every other group. It must not try to impose its views on others, nor can it press its own special interests to the point where they seriously endanger the interests of other groups or of the nation as a whole.

Furthermore, each group must exercise its implied veto with responsibility and discretion; and in times of great emergency it must forsake its veto right altogether. It dare not be intransigent or doctrinaire. It must make every conceivable effort to compromise, relying on its veto only as a last resort. For if any player wields this weapon recklessly, the game will break up—or all the other players will turn on him in anger, suspend the rules for the time being, and maul those very interests he is trying so desperately to protect. That was what happened in 1860, when the followers of Calhoun carried his doctrine to an unbearable extreme. Much the same thing, on a less violent scale, happened to American business interests in 1933 and to the labor unions in 1947.

This is the somewhat elusive sense, it seems to me, in which Calhoun's theory has been adopted by the American people. But elusive and subtle as it may be, it remains the basic rule of the game of politics in this country—and in this country alone. Nothing comparable exists in any other nation, although the British, in a different way, have applied their own rules of responsibility and self-restraint.

It is a rule which operates unofficially and entirely outside the Constitution—but it has given us a method by which all the official and Constitutional organs of government can be made to work. It also provides a means of selecting leaders on all levels of our political life, for hammering out policies, and for organizing and managing the conquest of political power.

The way in which this tradition works in practice can be observed most easily in Congress. Anyone who has ever tried to push through a piece of legislation quickly discovers that the basic units of organization on Capitol Hill are not the parties, but the so-called blocs, which are familiar to everyone who reads a newspaper. There are dozens of them—the farm bloc, the silver bloc, the friends of labor, the business group, the Midwestern isolationists, the public power bloc—and they all cut across party lines.

They are loosely organized and pretty blurred at the edges, so that every Congressman belongs at different times to several different blocs. Each of them represents a special interest group. Each of them ordinarily works hand-in-hand with that group's Washington lobby. In passing, it might be noted that these lobbies are by no means the cancerous growth which is sometimes pictured in civics textbooks. They have become an indispensable part of the political machine—the accepted channel through which American citizens make their wishes known and play their day-to-day role in the process of government. Nor is their influence measured solely by the size of the bankrolls and propaganda apparatus which they have at their disposal. Some of the smallest and poorest lobbies often are more effective than their well-heeled rivals. For example, Russell Smith, the one-man lobby of the Farmers Union, was largely responsible for conceiving and nursing through Congress the Employment Act of 1946, one of the most far-reaching measures adopted since the war.

Now it is an unwritten but firm rule of Congress that no important bloc shall ever be voted down—under normal circumstances—on any matter which touches its own vital interests. Each of them, in other words, has a tacit right of veto on legislation in which it is primarily concerned. The ultimate expression of this right is the institution—uniquely American—of the filibuster in the Senate. Recently it has acquired a bad name among liberals because the Southern conservatives have used it ruthlessly to fight off civil rights legislation and protect white supremacy. Not so long ago, however, the filibuster was the stoutest weapon of such men as Norris and the LaFollettes in defending many a progressive cause— and [in the future] the surviving handful of liberal Senators may well have occasion to use it again.

Naturally no bloc wants to exercise its veto power except when it is absolutely forced to—for this is a negative power, and one which is always subject to retaliation. Positive power to influence legislation, on the other hand, can be gained only by conciliation, compromise, and endless horse-trading.

The farm bloc, for instance, normally needs no outside aid to halt the passage of a hostile bill. As a last resort, three or four strong-lunged statesmen from the corn belt can always filibuster it to death in the Senate. If the bloc wants to put through a measure to support agricultural prices, however, it can succeed only by enlisting the help of other powerful special interest groups. Consequently, it must always be careful not to antagonize any potential ally by a reckless use of the veto; and it must be willing to pay for such help by throwing its support from time to time behind legislation sought by the labor bloc, the National Association of Manufacturers, or the school-teachers' lobby.

The classic alliance of this sort was formed in the early days of the New Deal, when most of the Roosevelt legislation was shoved onto the statute books by a temporary coalition of the farm bloc and urban labor, occasionally reinforced by such minor allies as the public power group and spokesmen for the northern Negroes. Mr. Roosevelt's political genius rested largely on his ability to put together a program which would offer something to each of these groups without fatally antagonizing any of them, and then to time the presentation of each bill so that he would always retain enough bargaining power to line up a Congressional majority. It also was necessary for him to avoid the veto of the business group, which viewed much of this legislation as a barbarous assault upon its privileges; and for this purpose he employed another traditional technique, which we shall examine a little later.

This process of trading blocs of votes is generally known as logrolling, and frequently it is deplored by the more innocent type of reformer. Such pious disapproval has no effect whatever on any practicing politician. He knows that log-rolling is a sensible and reasonably fair device, and that without it Congress could scarcely operate at all.

In fact, Congress gradually has developed a formal apparatus— the committee system—which is designed to make the log-rolling process as smooth and efficient as possible. There is no parallel system anywhere; the committees of Parliament and of the Continental legislative bodies work in an entirely different way.

Obviously the main business of Congress—the hammering out of a series of compromises between many special interest groups— cannot be conducted satisfactorily on the floor of the House or Senate. The meetings there are too large and far too public for such delicate negotiations. Moreover, every speech delivered on the floor must be aimed primarily at the voters back home, and not at the other members in the chamber. Therefore, Congress—especially the House—does nearly all its work in the closed sessions of its various committees, simply because the committee room is the only place where it is possible to arrange a compromise acceptable to all major interests affected.

For this reason, it is a matter of considerable importance to get a bill before the proper committee. Each committee serves as a forum for a particular cluster of special interests, and the assignment of a bill to a specific committee often decides which interest groups shall be recognized officially as affected by the measure and therefore entitled to a hand in its drafting. "Who is to have standing before the committee" is the technical term, and it is this decision that frequently decides the fate of the legislation. . . .

The stronghold of Calhoun's doctrine, however, is the American party—the wonder and despair of foreigners who cannot fit it into any of their concepts of political life.

The purpose of European parties is, of course, to divide men of different ideologies into coherent and disciplined organizations. The historic role of the American party, on the other hand, is not to divide but to unite. That task was imposed by simple necessity. If a division into ideological parties had been attempted, in addition to all the other centrifugal forces in this country, it very probably would have proved impossible to hold the nation together. The Founding Fathers understood this thoroughly; hence Washington's warning against "factions."

Indeed, on the one occasion when we did develop two ideological parties, squarely opposing each other on an issue of principle, the result was civil war. Fortunately, that was our last large-scale experiment with a third party formed on an ideological basis—for in its early days that is just what the Republican party was.

Its radical wing, led by such men as Thaddeus Stevens, Seward, and Chase, made a determined and skillful effort to substitute principles for interests as the foundations of American political life. Even within their own party, however, they were opposed by such practical politicians as Lincoln and Johnson—men who distrusted fanaticism in any form—and by the end of the Reconstruction period the experiment had been abandoned. American politics then swung back into its normal path and has never veered far away from it since. Although Calhoun's cause was defeated, his political theory came through the Civil War stronger than ever.

The result is that the American party has no permanent program and no fixed aim, except to win elections. Its one purpose is to unite the largest possible number of divergent interest groups in the pursuit of power. Its unity is one of compromise, not of dogma. It must—if it hopes to succeed—appeal to considerable numbers on both the left and the right, to rich and poor, Protestant and Catholic, farmer and industrial worker, native and foreign born.

It must be ready to bid for the support of any group that can deliver a sizable chunk of votes, accepting that group's pro-

gram with whatever modifications may be necessary to reconcile
the other members of the party. If sun worship, or Existentialism,
or the nationalization of industry should ever attract any significant
following in this country, you can be sure that both parties would
soon whip up a plank designed to win it over.

This ability to absorb new ideas (along with the enthusiasts
behind them) and to mold them into a shape acceptable to the
party's standpatters is, perhaps, the chief measure of vitality in
the party's leadership. Such ideas almost never germinate within
the party itself. They are stolen—very often from third parties. . . .

While each major party must always stand alert to grab a
promising new issue, it also must be careful never to scare off
any of the big, established interest groups. For as soon as it alien-
ates any one of them, it finds itself in a state of crisis.

For sixteen years the Republicans lost much of their standing
as a truly national party because they had made themselves
unacceptable to labor. Similarly, the Democrats, during the middle
stage of the New Deal, incurred the wrath of the business interests.
Ever since Mr. Truman was plumped into the White House, the
Democratic leadership has struggled desperately—though rather
ineptly—to regain the confidence of business men without at the
same time driving organized labor out of the ranks. It probably
would be safe to predict that if the Republican party is to regain
a long period of health, it must within the next four years make an
equally vigorous effort to win back the confidence of labor. For
the permanent veto of any major element in American society
means political death—as the ghosts of the Federalists and Whigs
can testify.

The weaknesses of the American political system are obvious—
much more obvious, in fact, than its virtues. These weaknesses
have been so sharply criticized for the past hundred years, by a
procession of able analysts ranging from Walter Bagehot to
Thomas K. Finletter, that it is hardly necessary to mention them
here. It is enough to note that most of the criticism has been aimed
at two major flaws.

First, it is apparent that the doctrine of the concurrent majority
is a negative one—a principle of inaction. A strong government,
capable of rapid and decisive action, is difficult to achieve under

a system which forbids it to do anything until virtually everybody acquiesces. In times of crisis, a dangerously long period of debate and compromise usually is necessary before any administration can carry out the drastic measures needed. The depression of the early thirties, the crisis in foreign policy which ended only with Pearl Harbor, the equally great crisis of the Marshall program . . . all illustrate this recurring problem.

This same characteristic of our system gives undue weight to the small but well-organized pressure group—especially when it is fighting *against* something. Hence a few power companies were able to block for twenty years the sensible use of the Muscle Shoals dam which eventually became the nucleus of TVA, and —in alliance with the railroads, rail unions, and Eastern port interests—they are still [in 1948] holding up development of the St. Lawrence Waterway. . . .

The negative character of our political rules also makes it uncommonly difficult for us to choose a President. Many of our outstanding political operatives—notably those who serve in the Senate—are virtually barred from a Presidential nomination because they are forced to get on record on too many issues. Inevitably they offend some important interest group, and therefore become "unavailable." Governors, who can keep their mouths shut on most national issues, have a much better chance to reach the White House. Moreover, the very qualities of caution and inoffensiveness which make a good candidate—Harding and Coolidge come most readily to mind—are likely to make a bad President.

An even more serious flaw in our scheme of politics is the difficulty in finding anybody to speak for the country as a whole. Calhoun would have argued that the national interest is merely the sum of all the various special interests, and therefore needs no spokesmen of its own—but in this case he clearly was wrong.

In practice, we tend to settle sectional and class conflicts at the expense of the nation as a whole—with results painful to all of us. The labor troubles in the spring of 1946, for instance, could be settled only on a basis acceptable to *both* labor and management: that is, on the basis of higher wages *plus* higher prices. The upshot was an inflationary spiral which is damaging everybody—and at this writing there is a good deal of mournful evidence that the process is about to be repeated. Countless other instances, from soil erosion to the rash of billboards along our highways, bear witness to the American tendency to neglect matters which are "only" of national interest, and therefore are left without a recognized sponsor.

Over the generations we have developed a series of practices and institutions which partly remedy these weaknesses, although we are still far from a complete cure. One such development has been the gradual strengthening of the Presidency as against Congress. As the only man elected by all the people, the President inevitably has had to take over many of the policy-making and leadership functions which the Founding Fathers originally assigned to the legislators. This meant, of course, that he could no longer behave merely as an obedient executor of the will of Congress, but was forced into increasingly frequent conflicts with Capitol Hill.

Today we have come to recognize that this conflict is one of the most important obligations of the Presidency. No really strong executive tries to avoid it—he accepts it as an essential part of his job. If he simply tries to placate the pressure groups which speak through Congress, history writes him down as a failure. For it is his duty to enlist the support of many minorities for measures rooted in the national interest, reaching beyond their own immediate concern—and, if necessary, to stand up against the ravening minorities for the interest of the whole.

In recent times this particular part of the President's job has been made easier by the growth of the Theory of Temporary Emergencies. All of us—or nearly all—have come around to admitting that in time of emergency special interest groups must forego their right of veto. As a result, the President often is tempted to scare up an emergency to secure legislation which could not be passed under any other pretext. Thus, most of the New Deal bills were introduced as "temporary emergency measures," although they were clearly intended to be permanent from the very first; for in no other way could Mr. Roosevelt avoid the veto of the business interests.

Again, in 1939 the threat of war enabled the President to push through much legislation which would have been impossible under normal circumstances. And Mr. Truman recently found it necessary to present the Greco-Turkish situation under the guise of a world crisis, in order to get authority and funds to carry out a rather small, routine police operation.

Because we have been so preoccupied with trying to patch up the flaws in our system, we have often overlooked its unique elements of strength. The chief of these is its ability to minimize conflict—not by suppressing the conflicting forces, but by absorbing and utilizing them. The result is a society which is both free and reasonably stable—a government which is as strong and effective as most dictatorships, but which can still adapt itself to social change.

The way in which the American political organism tames down the extremists of both the left and right is always fascinating to watch. Either party normally is willing to embrace any group or movement which can deliver votes—but in return it requires these groups to adjust their programs to fit the traditions, beliefs, and prejudices of the majority of the people. The fanatics, the implacable radicals cannot hope to get to first base in American politics until they abandon their fanaticism and learn the habits of conciliation. As a consequence, it is almost impossible for political movements here to become entirely irresponsible and to draw strength from the kind of demagogic obstruction which has nurtured both Communist and Fascist movements abroad.

The same process which gentles down the extremists also prods along the political laggards. As long as it is in a state of health, each American party has a conservative and a liberal wing. Sometimes one is dominant, sometimes the other—but even when the conservative element is most powerful, it must reckon with the left-wingers in its own family. At the moment [in 1948] the Republican party certainly is in one of its more conservative phases; yet it contains such men as Senators Morse, Aiken, Flanders, Tobey, and Baldwin, who are at least as progressive as most of the old New Dealers. They, and their counterparts in the Democratic party, exert a steady tug to the left which prevents either party from lapsing into complete reaction.

The strength of this tug is indicated by the fact that the major New Deal reforms have now been almost universally accepted. A mere ten years ago, the leading Republicans, plus many conservative Democrats, were hell-bent on wiping out social security, TVA, SEC, minimum-wage laws, rural electrification, and all the other dread innovations of the New Deal. Today no Presidential aspirant would dare suggest the repeal of a single one of them. In this country there simply is no place for a hard core of irreconcilable reactionaries, comparable to those political groups in France which have never yet accepted the reforms of the French Revolution.

This American tendency to push extremists of both the left and right toward a middle position has enabled us, so far, to escape class warfare. This is no small achievement for any political system; for class warfare cannot be tolerated by a modern industrial society. If it seriously threatens, it is bound to be suppressed by some form of totalitarianism, as it has been in Germany, Spain, Italy, Russia, and most of Eastern Europe. . . .

The uncompromising ideologist, of whatever faith, appears in our eyes peculiarly "un-American," simply because he cannot recognize the rule of the concurrent majority, nor can he accept the rules of mutual toleration which are necessary to make it work. Unless he forsakes his ideology, he cannot even understand that basic principle of American politics which was perhaps best expressed by Judge Learned Hand: "The spirit of liberty is the spirit which is not too sure that it is right."

RICHARD CURRENT

The Myth of the Concurrent Majority

Richard Current is Distinguished Professor of History at the University of North Carolina–Greensboro. Among his books are Old Thad Stevens *(1942);* Secretary Stimson *(1954); with J. G. Randall,* Lincoln the President: Last Full Measure *(1955); and* The Lincoln Nobody Knows *(1958). In the selection reprinted here from his recent biography of John C. Calhoun, Current challenges the position of writers like John Fischer and Peter Drucker who argue that Calhoun's principle of the concurrent majority is the key to the workings of the American political system.*

From Richard Current, *John C. Calhoun,* pp. 137–147. Copyright, ©, 1963 by Washington Square Press, Inc. Reprinted by permission of the publisher.

The Neo-Calhounism of the Twentieth Century

BY THE BEGINNING of the twentieth century, Calhoun had lost practically all relevance for living Americans. In 1911 the historian William E. Dodd, himself a Southerner, could write: "No political party looks back to Calhoun as its founder or rejuvenator, no group of public men proclaim allegiance to his doctrines, no considerable group of individuals outside of South Carolina profess any love for his name and ideals."

Suddenly, nearly a hundred years after his death, his reputation recovered and took on new aspects. By the middle of the twentieth century a Calhoun revival was under way. He and his theory seemed timely again.

New biographies came out: a three-volume, nearly definitive life; a "humanized" portrait that won a Pulitzer Prize; and a brief and critical "reappraisal." A book-length study of his political philosophy appeared. His *Disquisition on Government* was reissued again and again, in various editions. A project for publishing his complete writings, in twelve to fifteen volumes, was announced. He was made the subject of dozens of essays, and these were given space not only in learned journals but also in popular periodicals, among them *Harper's Magazine, Time,* and *The Saturday Evening Post.*

More remarkable than the quantity of this writing was the theme of much of it. The authors treated Calhoun as no antiquarian curiosity but a political philosopher with an enduring message and a unique relevance for their time.

The *Harper's* article (1948) asserted, strange though it might seem, that his theory "came through the Civil War stronger than ever." True, Calhoun had been concerned with a veto to protect the interests of slaveholders, but "by implication he would have given a similar veto to every other special interest, whether it be labor, management, the Catholic church, old-age pensioners, the silver miners, or the corn-growers of the Middle West." In a "somewhat elusive sense," the American people actually had adopted this concept of group veto and had put it into practice. "But elusive and subtle as it may be, it remains the basic rule of the game of politics in this country—and in this country alone." In short, Calhoun was the author of the "unwritten rules of American politics" as currently carried on. . . .

Writing in *The New York Times,* Senator Paul H. Douglas, of Illinois, reflected the new interpretation of Calhoun. It is "almost impossible to force through measures that are deeply resented and opposed by any large minority of the population," Douglas noted, in discussing the presidency. "This means that Calhoun's theory of requiring majorities of each significant group in the country to concur before a measure can be passed, while rejected in theory, has nevertheless been largely realized on important matters in practice."

These writers themselves had not rediscovered Calhoun; they were merely paraphrasing others, among them a political scientist, Peter F. Drucker, who had elaborated upon "Calhoun's pluralism" as a "key to American politics" in a professional journal (1948). Drucker contended that "for the constitutional veto power of the states over national legislation, by means of which Calhoun proposed to formalize the principle of sectional and interest compromise, was substituted in actual practice the much more powerful and much more elastic but extra-constitutional veto power of sections, interests, and pressure groups."

According to Drucker, this new veto power, the modern version of the concurrent majority, operated within Congress, the Administration, the national nominating convention, and, above all, the political party. In Congress there were blocs, such as the farm bloc, which could negative measures adversely affecting the groups they represented; and there were lobbies which could check legislation opposed by any of the major interests. In the Administration, some of the cabinet members, such as the secretaries of labor, agriculture, and commerce, looked out for the welfare of special groups. In the selection of a presidential candidate (and also of other candidates) availability or eligibility had to be taken into account: "Eligibility simply means that a candidate must not be unacceptable to any major interest, religious or regional group within the electorate; it is primarily a negative qualification." In the party—which "(rather than the states) has become the instrument to realize Calhoun's 'rule of the concurrent majority' "— the working of the veto was most in evidence: "It [the party] must, by definition, be acceptable equally to the right and the left, the rich and the poor, the farmer and the worker, the Protestant and the Catholic, the native and the foreign-born.". . .

In appraising the new interpretation, . . . two questions might be asked. First, does it, with reference to the "veto," accurately describe the political practices of the present? Second, does it really reflect the teachings of Calhoun a century and more ago?

The illustrations the neo-Calhounites use, to demonstrate the "veto" by each interest or each minority today, are plausible but unconvincing. Here is one: "For sixteen years [1932–48] the Republicans lost much of their standing as a truly national party because they had made themselves unacceptable to labor." Thus labor's "veto" did seem to have some effect during those years, but it failed to operate against the Taft-Hartley Act (1947), which the Republican Congress passed despite the last-ditch opposition of labor leaders, who denounced it as a "slave-labor law." And what had happened to labor's "veto" during the preceding twelve years of Republican supremacy? Another example: "Similarly, the Democrats during the middle stage of the New Deal incurred the wrath of the business interests." What became of the *business* "veto" during those sixteen (ultimately twenty) years that the New Dealers were in power? The explanation is offered that President Franklin D. Roosevelt had set aside the "veto" by his appeal to the needs of the "temporary emergency" which the depression had brought. But what does a "veto" amount to if it can be charmed away by a couple of magic words, such as "temporary emergency"? Surely this is not the kind of negative power that Calhoun had in mind!

A third illustration, which the neo-Calhounites use to support their argument, does further damage to their own case. "By 1946 . . . labor troubles could be resolved only on a basis acceptable to both labor and employer: higher wages *and* higher prices." Now, this may illustrate a "veto" by labor and by employer, but it also shows the lack, in this instance, of a "veto" by consumer or by farmer. What the wage-price agreement here amounts to, in fact, is a deal between two interests at the expense of the rest of the community. It is not an agreement arrived at through consultation of all interests.

No doubt this sort of bargaining *is* fairly typical of what actually goes on in the United States. Together with the other examples mentioned, it demonstrates the fact that politicians and pressure groups normally do not appease every minority (not even every big one), do not allow each interest a "veto," do not arrive at action on the basis of unanimity. Instead, they construct a working majority through the combination of several (but not necessarily all) minorities. When, to form the combination, the support of a particular group is needed, the demands of that group, the positive or negative demands, are respected. To the extent, then, that any interest or minority can get concessions from other inter-

ests or minorities in the process of forming the majority, to that
extent the "veto" of the interest or minority is effective. But only
to that extent. The process is familiar enough, and so is the word
for it—"logrolling."

This practice is far from new in the history of American politics.
In Calhoun's own time there were blocs, lobbies, and factions,
and there was logrolling among them. Calhoun himself was aware,
painfully aware, of the concessions that both Whig and Democratic
politicians were prone to make to tariff lobbyists or to the anti-
slavery or free-soil bloc. He knew from bitter experience what
"availability" meant in the choosing of a presidential candidate.
He was acquainted with the struggle, essentially the same then as
now, by which contending groups sought to get control of the
government. "If no one interest be strong enough, of itself, to
obtain it," he wrote, "a combination will be formed between those
whose interests are most alike—each conceding something to the
others, until a sufficient number is obtained to make a majority."
That was the essence of the process in his day, and it remains the
essence of the process in ours.

But this was not and is not what Calhoun advocated. Quite the
contrary. He condemned that kind, the familiar kind, of politics.
He thought that by its inevitable tendency "principle and policy
would lose all influence in the elections; then cunning, falsehood,
deception, slander, fraud, and gross appeals to the appetites of
the lowest and most worthless portions of the community would
take the place of sound reason and wise debate." Certainly he
had no use for the kind of trading that went on at party conventions. He opposed allowing minorities, such as the abolitionists,
to exercise any kind of veto on presidential nominations. . . .

Calhoun went on to denounce all nominating conventions as
"irresponsible bodies" which were unknown to the Constitution.
He urged Southerners to renounce the forthcoming Democratic
convention of 1848 and to unite in a strictly Southern party. The
election of the President, he added, ought to be left strictly to the
electoral college, as the framers of the Constitution had intended.
He refused to be satisfied with the combination of interests upon
policy unless *all* interests (that is, all property-owning interests
and, in particular, the slavery interest) were consulted and their
approval gained. "I am," he declared, "in favor of the government of the whole; the only really and truly popular government—

a government based on the concurrent majority—the joint assent of all the parts, through their respective majority of the whole." He insisted upon essential *unanimity* as the condition for governmental action.

This requirement, for all the assertions of the neo-Calhounites, does not exist today. It did not exist when Calhoun was alive. He looked for some means of imposing it; he found the means, constitutionally, in his theory of state rights and, politically, in his plan for creating a sectional party or at least a sectional faction— the solid South. Except when his own presidential hopes were active and his own chances appeared to be good, he was inclined to turn away from the game of politics as it was customarily played—and still is.

In sum, the new interpreters of Calhoun have been careless in their reading of his philosophy and superficial in their description of current politics. They have attributed to him the very political principles and practices which he detested and for which he sought quite different alternatives. Without realizing it, they have misused the term "concurrent majority" so as to make it mean essentially what he himself meant by the term "numerical majority," that is, a combination of the majorities of many or even most *but not all* interests.

It might, or might not, be a good thing if the United States actually had institutions to give effect to the kind of "political pluralism" that the neo-Calhounites admire. It might be desirable, for instance, to set up a third house as a supplement to Congress, a third house in which economic, sectional, religious, racial, and other groups would be represented as such; and in which each of them could exercise a veto. Possibly this would work, and possibly it could be considered as a Calhounian solution—but only if certain passages are isolated from his works, unrestrained inferences are drawn from these passages, and the rest of his writings and his career itself are ignored.

On the whole, he seems to have taken a dualist, not a pluralist, view of politics. Though he mentioned the existence of various interests in society, he made no attempt to list and describe them, and certainly he never specified racial or religious minorities, or the working class, as deserving of the veto power. Generally he ignored the variety of possible groupings. When he got down to theorizing, he really thought about only two groups at a time, not several. On occasion he dealt with the duality of capital and labor.

Most often he had in mind the twofold grouping of North against South, free states against slave states. These were, to him, the majority and the minority, and this was the minority he sought to protect—the minority of slaveholders.

It is farfetched to say that his "insights remain vital for any minority." This might be remotely true if his theory were abstracted enough, but the theory would have to be stretched to the point where it had only the most tenuous connection with what Calhoun actually thought and said. The assumption would have to be made that, somehow, the case for the onetime master has been, or at least can be, converted into a case for the onetime slave. This assumption has yet to be proved. Perhaps the National Association for the Advancement of Colored People ought to peruse Calhoun's works for means of protecting Negro rights. If the N.A.A.C.P. should do so, the news would be startling, and if the search were successful, the news would be amazing.

Surely the spirit of Calhoun is not to be found in the meetings of today's minority groups, of whatever creed or color. Nor is it to be discovered in all the political bargaining of the lobby, the congressional bloc, the executive department, or the smoke-filled room. We of the twentieth century must look elsewhere if we are to find the genuine ghost of the Great Nullifier.

ROBERT A. DAHL

A Multiplicity of Check-Points

Robert Dahl, in this second selection from his most recent book, constructs a pluralist model of the normal workings of the American political system. Since the student has already encountered one type of pluralist analysis in the article by Fischer, he should keep in mind that not all pluralist approaches are alike (any more than all elite dominance analyses are alike) and should be on the alert to note the differences between Fischer and Dahl.

From Robert A. Dahl, *Pluralist Democracy in the United States: Conflict and Consent,* pp. 325–329. Copyright 1967 by Rand McNally and Company. Reprinted by permission of the publisher.

Periods of Moderate Conflict

IF YOU WERE TO PICK at random any year in American history since the Constitutional Convention to illustrate the workings of the political system, you would stand a rather good chance of being able to describe American politics during that year as follows:

Important government policies would be arrived at through negotiation, bargaining, persuasion, and pressure at a considerable number of different sites in the political system—the White House, the bureaucracies, the labyrinth of committees in Congress, the federal and state courts, the state legislatures and executives, the local governments. No single organized political interest, party, class, region, or ethnic group would control all of these sites.

Different individuals and groups would not all exert an equal influence on decisions about government policies. The extent of influence individuals or groups exerted would depend on a complex set of factors: their political skills, how aroused and active they were, their numbers, and their access to such political resources as organization, money, connections, propaganda, etc. People who lacked even suffrage and had no other resources—slaves, for example—would of course be virtually powerless. But because *almost* every group has some political resources—at a minimum, the vote—most people who felt that their interests were significantly affected by a proposed change in policy would have some influence in negotiations.

All the important political forces—particularly all the candidates and elected officials of the two major parties—would accept (or at any rate would not challenge) the legitimacy of the basic social, economic, and political structures of the United States. Organized opposition to these basic structures would be confined to minority movements too feeble to win representation in Congress or a single electoral vote for their presidential candidate.

Political conflict would be moderate.

Changes in policies would be marginal. . . .

A Multiplicity of Check-Points

When one looks at American political institutions in their entirety and compares them with institutions in other democracies, what stands out as a salient feature is the extraordinary variety of opportunities these institutions provide for an organized minority to block, modify, or delay a policy which the minority opposes. Consequently, it is a rarity for any coalition to carry out its policies without having to bargain, negotiate, and compromise with its opponents; often, indeed, it wins a victory in one institution only to suffer defeat in another.

The multiplicity of check-points that American political institutions provide organized minorities result from three inter-related factors. First, there is a great diversity of political institutions. Second, among these institutions there is no clear-cut hierarchy of legal and constitutional authority. Third, there is no *de facto* hierarchy of power.

The President, the House, and the Senate are separate institutions. Each reposes on a separate and different system of elections with different terms of office and different electorates. Groups weighty in a presidential election may be much weaker in House and Senate elections. The policies of a particular group or coalition may be supported in one institution and opposed in another. In many areas of policy, each of these major institutions has a veto over the others. Each has a reservoir of legal, constitutional, and *de facto* power.

Neither the Executive, the House, nor the Senate is monolithic. A group may be strong in one executive agency, weak in another; strong in a particular House or Senate committee, weak elsewhere. A group may have individual spokesmen and opponents located at various places in the executive agencies, the regulatory commissions, the House, the Senate, the standing committees, a conference committee.

The political parties are themselves coalitions. Nominations are not centrally controlled. National party leaders have limited resources for influencing their members in Congress. A minority may be defeated at the presidential nominating convention, yet retain its strength in state and local party organizations; it cannot be pushed aside.

Again and again in the history of the Supreme Court, a minority coalition that could not win the Presidency or majorities in Congress has preserved a majority within the Supreme Court to fight a rear-guard delaying action. Chief Justice John Marshall fought Thomas Jefferson. In the Dred Scott case, Chief Justice Roger B. Taney, fearing what future majorities might do, fought to preserve dead or dying ones. Embattled minorities entrenched in the Court knocked out the income tax in 1894, child labor laws in 1918 and 1922, New Deal reforms from 1935 to 1937. In its epochal decision on school integration in 1954, the Court pronounced policy that could not possibly have passed through Congress at that time. Even if they rarely win their wars in the Congress, minorities well represented on the Court can win some impressive battles.

Even when minorities lose in national politics, they still may win in the states. Although defeated in [the] Civil War, the white South nonetheless forced the North to concede white supremacy, thanks in considerable measure to the institutions of federalism. In the North, trade unions and advocates of factory reform, abolition of child labor, workmen's compensation, shorter hours, protection of women workers won in the state legislatures what they could not win nationally without the agreement of President, Congress, and Court. The principle holds even within the states, where legislative, executive, and judicial institutions follow the pattern of the national government, though often with greater fragmentation. Local governments provide still other check-points.

Neither the Constitution, constitutional doctrine, nor American ideology have ever treated all these institutions, national and federal, as components of an ordered hierarchy in which some constitutional units are invariably subordinate to others. Constitutionally speaking, the President does not dominate Congress; nor, on the other hand, is the President a mere agent of Congress; the Senate is not constitutionally superior to the House, nor Congress and President to the Judiciary, nor the governors and state legislatures to the President and Congress.

Nor do Americans agree, as we have already seen, on any single principle of legitimate decision-making that would provide a way of ordering these institutions into a lawful hierarchy. Majority-rule? Yes, but which majority? Operating in what institution? By what means? And anyway what of minority rights? Given varying interpretations of political legitimacy possible within the American tradition, the extent to which a particular principle or institution is upheld often depends on whose ox is being gored. In the 1930's, liberals attacked the Supreme Court and defended majority rule; in the 1950's and 1960's, the prestige of the Court among liberals had never been higher. During the early years of the New Deal, conservatives saw the Court as a bastion of freedom; in the 1950's some of them came to view it as rather tyrannical. During the

New Deal and the Fair Deal, liberal Democrats frequently extolled the virtues (and political legitimacy) of a strong President; with the election of a Republican President in 1952 they began to discover new virtues in Congress; but that theme was quickly muted after 1960. Many conservatives insist that "power must be kept close to the people"; they praise the legitimacy of "states' rights"; but they oppose attempts to bring power "closer to the people" by re-apportioning state legislatures or allowing Negroes to vote.

To be sure, there is the belief in the final legitimacy of rule by the people: that "this country, with its institutions, belongs to the people who inhabit it," as Lincoln said. "Whenever they shall grow weary of the existing government, they can exercise their constitutional right of amending it, or their revolutionary right to dismember or overthrow it." Yet the "people" have not chosen to amend the Constitution in order to establish a single hierarchy of authority in our political institutions. Quite the contrary: "The people" have never shown the slightest interest in any of the schemes for doing so that are sometimes propounded by eager constitution-makers. Moreover, a *majority* of the people is not constitutionally sovereign even in amending the Constitution, unless that majority happens also to constitute a majority in three fourths of the states. Indeed, a unanimity of opinion in three fourths of the states does not make "the people" constitutionally sovereign even in its power to amend the Constitution in at least one respect; for the final words of Article V of the Constitution read as follows: ". . . no state, without its consent, shall be deprived of its equal suffrage in the Senate."

To anyone searching for a single principle of legitimate decision-making, it is of little value to say that "the people" may exercise "their revolutionary right to dismember or overthrow" the political institutions. Perhaps if Americans converged on a single principle it would be this: Unanimity, though unattainable, is best; institutions must therefore be so contrived that they will compel a constant search for the highest attainable degree of consent.

If in constitutional theory there is no hierarchy of legitimate authorities, then fact . . . conforms with theory. That the President is no mere agent of the Congress; that the Congress is not subordinate to the President; that neither the federal government nor a state is subordinate to the other on all matters—these are facts of political life, facts doubly resistant to change because fact corresponds to constitutional doctrine and American ideology.

The institutions, then, offer organized minorities innumerable sites in which to fight, perhaps to defeat, at any rate to damage an opposing coalition. Consequently, the institutions place a high premium on strategies of compromise and conciliation, on a search for consensus. They inhibit and delay change until there is wide support; they render comprehensive change unlikely; they foster incremental adjustments. They generate politicians who learn how to deal gently with opponents, who struggle endlessly in building and holding coalitions together, who doubt the possibilities of great change, who seek compromises.

C. WRIGHT MILLS

The Power Elite

C. Wright Mills was Professor of Sociology at Columbia University until his untimely death in 1962. Among his books are White Collar *(1951);* The Power Elite *(1956);* The Causes of World War III *(1958);* The Sociological Imagination *(1959);* Listen, Yankee *(1960); and* Power, Politics, and People: The Collected Essays of C. Wright Mills, *edited by I. L. Horowitz (1963). The following selection from an article addressed to a British audience summarizes the analysis of American politics and society developed in* The Power Elite.

THE POWER TO MAKE DECISIONS of national and international consequence is now so clearly seated in political, military, and economic institutions that other areas of society seem off to the side and, on occasion, readily subordinated to these. The scattered institutions of religion, education and family are increasingly shaped by the big three, in which history-making decisions now regularly occur. Behind this fact there is all the push and drive of a fabulous technology; for these three institutional orders have incorporated

From *Power, Politics, and People: The Collected Essays of C. Wright Mills,* pp. 32–41, edited by Irving Louis Horowitz. Copyright © 1963 by the Estate of C. Wright Mills. Reprinted by permission of Oxford University Press, Inc.

this technology and now guide it, even as it shapes and paces their development.

As each has assumed its modern shape, its effects upon the other two have become greater, and the traffic between the three has increased. There is no longer, on the one hand, an economy, and, on the other, a political order, containing a military establishment unimportant to politics and to money-making. There is a political economy numerously linked with military order and decision. This triangle of power is now a structural fact, and it is the key to any understanding of the higher circles in America today. For as each of these domains has coincided with the others, as decisions in each have become broader, the leading men of each—the high military, the corporation executives, the political directorate—have tended to come together to form the power elite of America.

The political order, once composed of several dozen states with a weak federal-center, has become an executive apparatus which has taken up into itself many powers previously scattered, legislative as well as administrative, and which now reaches into all parts of the social structure. The long-time tendency of business and government to become more closely connected has since World War II reached a new point of explicitness. Neither can now be seen clearly as a distinct world. The growth of executive government does not mean merely the "enlargement of government" as some kind of autonomous bureaucracy: under American conditions, it has meant the ascendancy of the corporation man into political eminence. Already during the New Deal, such men had joined the political directorate; as of World War II they came to dominate it. Long involved with government, now they have moved into quite full direction of the economy of the war effort and of the post-war era.

The economy, once a great scatter of small productive units in somewhat automatic balance, has become internally dominated by a few hundred corporations, administratively and politically interrelated, which together hold the keys to economic decision. This economy is at once a permanent-war economy and a private-corporation economy. The most important relations of the corporation to the state now rest on the coincidence between military and corporate interests, as defined by the military and the corporate rich, and accepted by politicians and public. Within the elite as a whole, this coincidence of military domain and corporate realm strengthens both of them and further subordinates the merely political man. Not the party politician, but the corporation executive, is now more likely to sit with the military to answer the question: what is to be done?

The military order, once a slim establishment in a context of civilian distrust, has become the largest and most expensive feature of government; behind smiling public relations, it has all the grim and clumsy efficiency of a great and sprawling bureaucracy. The high military have gained decisive political and economic relevance. The seemingly permanent military threat places a premium upon them and virtually all political and economic actions are now judged in terms of military definitions of reality: the higher military have ascended to a firm position within the power elite of our time.

In part at least this is a result of an historical fact, pivotal for the years since 1939: the attention of the elite has shifted from domestic problems—centered in the 'thirties around slump—to international problems—centered in the 'forties and 'fifties around war. By long historical usage, the government of the United States has been shaped by domestic clash and balance; it does not have suitable agencies and traditions for the democratic handling of international affairs. In considerable part, it is in this vacuum that the power elite has grown.

(i) To understand the unity of this power elite, we must pay attention to the psychology of its several members in their respective milieux. In so far as the power elite is composed of men of similar origin and education, of similar career and style of life, their unity may be said to rest upon the fact that they are of similar social type, and to lead to the fact of their easy intermingling. This kind of unity reaches its frothier apex in the sharing of that prestige which is to be had in the world of the celebrity. It achieves a more solid culmination in the fact of the interchangeability of positions between the three dominant institutional orders. It is revealed by considerable traffic of personnel within and between these three, as well as by the rise of specialized go-betweens as in the new style high-level lobbying.

(ii) Behind such psychological and social unity are the structure and the mechanics of those institutional hierarchies over which the political directorate, the corporate rich, and the high military now preside. How each of these hierarchies is shaped and what relations it has with the others determine in large part the relations of their rulers. Were these hierarchies scattered and disjointed, then their respective elites might tend to be scattered and disjointed; but if they have many interconnections and points of coinciding interest, then their elites tend to form a coherent kind of grouping. The unity of the elite is not a simple reflection of the unity of institutions, but men and institutions are always related; that is why we must understand the elite today in connection with such institutional trends as the development of a permanent-war establishment, alongside a privately incorporated economy, inside a virtual political vacuum. For the men at the top have been selected and formed by such institutional trends.

(iii) Their unity, however, does not rest solely upon psychological similarity and social intermingling, nor entirely upon the structural blending of commanding positions and common interests. At times it is the unity of a more explicit co-ordination.

To say that these higher circles are increasingly co-ordinated, that this is *one* basis of their unity, and that at times—as during open war—such co-ordination is quite wilful, is not to say that the co-ordination is total or continuous, or even that it is very surefooted. Much less is it to say that the power elite has emerged as the realization of a plot. Its rise cannot be adequately explained in any psychological terms.

Yet we must remember that institutional trends may be defined as opportunities by those who occupy the command posts. Once such opportunities are recognized, men may avail themselves of them. Certain types of men from each of these three areas, more far-sighted than others, have actively promoted the liaison even before it took its truly modern shape. Now more have come to see that their several interests can more easily be realized if they work together, in informal as well as in formal ways, and accordingly they have done so.

The idea of the power elite is of course an interpretation. It rests upon and it enables us to make sense of major institutional trends, the social similarities and psychological affinities of the men at the top. But the idea is also based upon what has been happening on the middle and lower levels of power, to which I now turn.

There are of course other interpretations of the American system of power. The most usual is that it is a moving balance of many competing interests. The image of balance, at least in America, is derived from the idea of the economic market: in the nineteenth century, the balance was thought to occur between a great scatter of individuals and enterprises; in the twentieth century, it is thought to occur between great interest blocs. In both views, the politician is the key man of power because he is the broker of many conflicting powers.

I believe that the balance and the compromise in American society—the "countervailing powers" and the "veto groups," of parties and associations, of strata and unions—must now be seen as having mainly to do with the middle levels of power. It is these middle levels that the political journalist and the scholar of politics are most likely to understand and to write about—if only because, being mainly middle class themselves, they are closer to them. Moreover these levels provide the noisy content of most "political" news and gossip; the images of these levels are more or less in accord with the folklore of how democracy works; and, if the master-image of balance is accepted, many intellectuals, especially in their current patrioteering, are readily able to satisfy such political optimism as they wish to feel. Accordingly, liberal interpretations of what is happening in the United States are now virtually the only interpretations that are widely distributed.

But to believe that the power system reflects a balancing society is, I think, to confuse the present era with earlier times, and to confuse its top and bottom with its middle levels.

By the top levels, as distinguished from the middle, I intend to refer, first of all, to the scope of the decisions that are made. At the top today, these decisions have to do with all the issues of war and peace. They have also to do with slump and poverty which are now so very much problems of international scope. I intend also to refer to whether or not the groups that struggle politically have a chance to gain the positions from which such top decisions are made, and indeed whether their members do usually hope for such top national command. Most of the competing interests which make up the clang and clash of American politics are strictly concerned with their slice of the existing pie. Labor unions, for example, certainly have no policies of an international sort other than those which given unions adopt for the strict economic protection of their members. Neither do farm organizations. The actions of such middle-level powers may indeed have consequence for top-level policy; certainly at times they hamper these policies. But they are not truly concerned with them, which means of course that their influence tends to be quite irresponsible.

The facts of the middle levels may in part be understood in terms of the rise of the power elite. The expanded and centralized and interlocked hierarchies over which the power elite preside have encroached upon the old balance and relegated it to the middle level. But there are also independent developments of the middle levels. These, it seems to me, are better understood as an affair of intrenched and provincial demands than as a center of national decision. As such, the middle level often seems much more of a stalemate than a moving balance.

(i) The middle level of politics is not a forum in which there are debated the big decisions of national and international life. Such debate is not carried on by nationally responsible parties representing and clarifying alternative policies. There are no such parties in the United States. More and more, fundamental issues never come to any point or decision before the Congress, much less before the electorate in party campaigns. In the case of Formosa, in the spring of 1955, the Congress abdicated all debate concerning events and decisions which surely bordered on war. The same is largely true of the 1957 crisis in the Middle East. Such decisions now regularly by-pass the Congress and are never clearly focused issues for public decision.

The American political campaign distracts attention from national and international issues, but that is not to say that there are no issues in these campaigns. In each district and state, issues are set up and watched by organized interests of sovereign local importance. The professional politician is of course a party politician, and the two parties are semi-feudal organizations: they trade patronage and other favors for votes and for protection. The differences between them, so far as national issues are concerned, are very narrow and very mixed up. Often each seems to be forty-eight parties, one to each state; and accordingly, the politician as campaigner and as Congressman is not concerned with national party lines, if any are discernible. Often he is not subject to any effective national party discipline. He speaks for the interests of his own constituency, and he is concerned with national issues only insofar as they affect the interests effectively organized there, and hence his chances of re-election. That is why, when he does speak of national matters, the result is so often such an empty rhetoric. Seated in his sovereign locality, the politician is not at the national summit. He is on and of the middle levels of power.

(ii) Politics is not an arena in which free and independent organizations truly connect the lower and middle levels of society with the top levels of decision. Such organizations are not an effective and major part of American life today. As more people are drawn into the political arena, their associations become mass in scale, and the power of the individual becomes dependent upon them; to the extent that they are effective, they have become larger, and to that extent they have become less accessible to the influence of the individual. This is a central fact about associations in any mass society: it is of most consequence for political parties and for trade unions.

In the 'thirties, it often seemed that labor would become an insurgent power independent of corporation and state. Organized labor was then emerging for the first time on an American scale, and the only political sense of direction it needed was the slogan, "organize the unorganized." Now without the mandate of the slump, labor remains without political direction. Instead of economic and political struggles it has become deeply entangled in administrative routines with both corporation and state. One of its major functions, as a vested interest of the new society, is the regulation of such irregular tendencies as may occur among the rank and file.

There is nothing, it seems to me, in the make-up of the current labor leadership to allow us to expect that it can or that it will lead, rather than merely react. In so far as it fights at all it fights over a share of the goods of a single way of life and not over that way of life itself. The typical labor leader in the U.S.A. today is better understood as an adaptive creature of the main business drift than as an independent actor in a truly national context.

(iii) The idea that this society is a balance of powers requires us to assume that the units in balance are of more or less equal power and that they are truly independent of one another. These assumptions have rested, it seems clear, upon the historical importance of a large and independent middle class. In the latter nineteenth century and during the Progressive Era, such a class of farmers and small businessmen fought politically—and lost—their last struggle for a paramount role in national decision. Even then, their aspirations seemed bound to their own imagined past.

This old, independent middle class has of course declined. On the most generous count, it is now 40 per cent of the total middle class (at most 20 per cent of the total labor force). Moreover, it has become politically as well as economically dependent upon the state, most notably in the case of the subsidized farmer.

The *new* middle class of white-collar employees is certainly not the political pivot of any balancing society. It is in no way politically unified. Its unions, such as they are, often serve merely to incorporate it as hanger-on of the labor interest. For a considerable period, the old middle class *was* an independent base of power; the new middle class cannot be. Political freedom and economic security *were* anchored in small and independent properties; they are not anchored in the worlds of the white-collar job. Scattered property holders were economically united by more or less free markets; the jobs of the new middle class are integrated by corporate authority. Economically, the white-collar classes are in the same condition as wage workers; politically, they are in a worse condition, for they are not organized. They are no vanguard of historic change; they are at best a rear guard of the welfare state.

The agrarian revolt of the 'nineties, the small-business revolt that has been more or less continuous since the 'eighties, the labor revolt of the 'thirties—each of these has failed as an independent movement which could countervail against the powers that be; they have failed as politically autonomous third parties. But they have succeeded, in varying degree, as interests vested in the expanded corporation and state; they have succeeded as parochial interests seated in particular districts, in local divisions of the two parties, and in the Congress. What they would become, in short, are well-established features of the *middle* levels of balancing power, on which we may now observe all those strata and interests which in the course of American history have been defeated in their bids for top power or which have never made such bids.

Fifty years ago many observers thought of the American state as a mask behind which an invisible government operated. But nowadays much of what was called the old lobby, visible or invisible, is part of the quite visible government. The "governmentalization of the lobby" has proceeded in both the legislative and the executive domain, as well as between them. The executive bureauc-

racy becomes not only the center of decision but also the arena
within which major conflicts of power are resolved or denied resolution. "Administration" replaces electoral politics; the maneuvering
of cliques (which include leading senators as well as civil servants)
replaces the open clash of parties.

The shift of corporation men into the political directorate has
accelerated the decline of the politicians in the Congress to the
middle levels of power; the formation of the power elite rests in
part upon this relegation. It rests also upon the semi-organized
stalemate of the interests of sovereign localities, into which the
legislative function has so largely fallen; upon the virtually complete absence of a civil service that is a politically neutral, but politically relevant, depository of brain-power and executive skill;
and it rests upon the increased official secrecy behind which great
decisions are made without benefit of public or even of Congressional debate.

There is one last belief upon which liberal observers everywhere
base their interpretations and rest their hopes. That is the idea of
the public and the associated idea of public opinion. Conservative
thinkers, since the French Revolution, have of course Viewed With
Alarm the rise of the public, which they have usually called the
masses, or something to that effect. "The populace is sovereign,"
wrote Gustave Le Bon, "and the tide of barbarism mounts." But
surely those who have supposed the masses to be well on their
way to triumph are mistaken. In our time, the influence of publics
or of masses within political life is in fact decreasing, and such
influence as on occasion they do have tends, to an unknown but
increasing degree, to be guided by the means of mass communication.

In a society of publics, discussion is the ascendant means of
communication, and the mass media, if they exist, simply enlarge
and animate this discussion, linking one face-to-face public with
the discussions of another. In a mass society, the dominant type
of communication is the formal media, and publics become mere
markets for these media: the "public" of a radio program consists of all those exposed to it. When we try to look upon the United
States today as a society of publics, we realize that it has moved a
considerable distance along the road to the mass society.

In official circles, the very term, "the public," has come to have
a phantom meaning, which dramatically reveals its eclipse. The

deciding elite can identify some of those who clamor publicly as "Labor," others as "Business," still others as "Farmer." But these are not the public. "The public" consists of the unidentified and the non-partisan in a world of defined and partisan interests. In this faint echo of the classic notion, the public is composed of these remnants of the old and new middle classes whose interests are not explicitly defined, organized, or clamorous. . . .

All this is indeed far removed from the eighteenth-century idea of the public of public opinion. That idea parallels the economic idea of the magical market. Here is the market composed of freely competing entrepreneurs; there is the public composed of circles of people in discussion. As price is the result of anonymous, equally weighted, bargaining individuals, so public opinion is the result of each man's having thought things out for himself and then contributing his voice to the great chorus. To be sure, some may have more influence on the state of opinion than others, but no one group monopolizes the discussion, or by itself determines the opinions that prevail.

In this classic image, the people are presented with problems. They discuss them. They formulate viewpoints. These viewpoints are organized, and they compete. One viewpoint "wins out." Then the people act on this view, or their representatives are instructed to act it out, and this they promptly do.

Such are the images of democracy which are still used as working justifications of power in America. We must now recognize this description as more a fairy tale than a useful approximation. The issues that now shape man's fate are neither raised nor decided by any public at large. The idea of a society that is at bottom composed of publics is not a matter of fact; it is the proclamation of an ideal, and as well the assertion of a legitimation masquerading as fact.

I cannot here describe the several great forces within American society as well as elsewhere which have been at work in the debilitation of the public. I want only to remind you that publics, like free associations, can be deliberately and suddenly smashed, or they can more slowly wither away. But whether smashed in a week or withered in a generation, the demise of the public must be seen in connection with the rise of centralized organizations, with all their new means of power, including those of the mass media of distraction. These, we now know, often seem to expropriate the rationality and the will of the terrorized or—as the case may be—the voluntarily indifferent society of masses. In the more democratic process of indifference the remnants of such publics as remain may only occasionally be intimidated by fanatics in search of "disloyalty." But regardless of that, they lose their will for decision because they do not possess the instruments for decision; they lose their sense of political belonging because they do not belong; they lose their political will because they see no way to realize it.

The political structure of a modern democratic state requires that such a public as is projected by democratic theorists not only exist but that it be the very forum within which a politics of real issues is enacted.

It requires a civil service that is firmly linked with the world of knowledge and sensibility, and which is composed of skilled men who, in their careers and in their aspirations, are truly independent of any private, which is to say, corporation, interests.

It requires nationally responsible parties which debate openly and clearly the issues which the nation, and indeed the world, now so rigidly confronts.

It requires an intelligentsia, inside as well as outside the universities, who carry on the big discourse of the western world, and whose work is relevant to and influential among parties and movements and publics.

And it certainly requires, as a fact of power, that there be free associations standing between families and smaller communities and publics, on the one hand, and the state, the military, the corporation, on the other. For unless these do exist, there are no vehicles for reasoned opinion, no instruments for the rational exertion of public will.

Such democratic formations are not now ascendant in the power structure of the United States, and accordingly the men of decision are not men selected and formed by careers within such associations and by their performance before such publics. The top of modern American society is increasingly unified, and often seems wilfully co-ordinated: at the top there has emerged an elite whose power probably exceeds that of any small group of men in world history. The middle levels are often a drifting set of stalemated forces: the middle does not link the bottom with the top. The bottom of this society is politically fragmented, and even as a passive fact, increasingly powerless: at the bottom there is emerging a mass society.

TALCOTT PARSONS

The Distribution of Power in American Society

Talcott Parsons, Professor of Sociology at Harvard University, is one of the more influential figures in contemporary social science. The bibliography of his books is vast. Representative are The Structure of Social Action (*1937*), The Social System (*1951*), Essays in Sociological Theory (*revised 1959*), Structure and Process in Modern Societies (*1959*), Social Structure and Personality (*1964*), *and* Societies: Evolutionary and Comparative Perspectives (*1966*). *The following selection is from an extended critical review of C. Wright Mills's* The Power Elite. *Parsons and Mills were far apart both in their approaches to sociology and in their empirical findings about American politics and society.*

THE MILLS ANALYSIS presents what, to me, is a subtle and complex combination of acceptable and unacceptable elements. Let me now attempt, at some of the most important points, to unravel these elements from each other. I want to try this first on the level of empirical generalization and then to raise one or two more strictly theoretical problems. I shall do so more in my own terms than in those employed by Mills.

In my opinion, two salient sets of processes have been going on in American society during the past half-century, the combination of which encompasses the main facts which are essential to our problem. The first of these is the dynamic of a maturing industrial society, including not only the highly industrialized economy itself but its setting in the society as a whole—notably, its political system and class structure (in a wider sense of the term "class" than Mills')—and the repercussions of the industrial development on

From Talcott Parsons, "The Distribution of Power in American Society," *World Politics*, X (October, 1957), 128–139. Reprinted by permission of *World Politics*.

the rest of the society. The second concerns the altered position of the United States in world society, which is a consequence in part of our own economic growth, in part of a variety of exogenous changes, including the relative decline of the Western European powers, the rise of Soviet Russia, and the break-up of the "colonial" organization of much of the non-white world. The enormous enhancement of American power and responsibility in the world has taken place in a relatively short time and was bound to have profound repercussions on the characteristics of our own society. Our old political isolation has disappeared and given way to the deepest of involvements.

My first thesis is that these two processes *both* work in the direction of increasing the relative importance of government in our society and, with it, of political power. But their impact has been all the greater because of the extent to which the United States has been an almost specifically non-political society. This has been evidenced above all in the institutions and tradition of political decentralization already mentioned, one aspect of which is the localism which Mills discusses. A second, however, has been a cultural tradition which has emphasized economic values—an emphasis on enterprise and production in an activist sense, not a merely passive hedonistic valuation of the enjoyment of material well-being. Moreover, the virtually unimpeded process of settlement of a continent in political isolation from the main system of world powers has favored maintenance of this emphasis to a greater extent than would otherwise have readily been possible.

At some points in his discussion, Mills seems to look back to the Jeffersonian picture of a system of economic production consisting mainly of small farmers and artisans, with presumably a small mercantile class mediating between them and consumers. . . .

In all salient respects, the modern economy has moved very far from the Jeffersonian ideal. The pace-setting units have become both large and specialized. Their development has been part of a general process of structural differentiation in the society which has led to greater specialization in many fields. An essential aspect of the process of development of the economy as a system in *both* these senses is greater specialization on at least three levels: first, the specialization of organizations in the functions of economic production as distinguished from other functions; second, the specialization of functions within the economy; and third, the specialization of the roles of classes of individuals within the organization.

Leadership is an essential function in all social systems, which with their increase of scale and their functional differentiation tend to become more specialized. I think we can, within considerable limits, regard the emergence of the large firm with operations on a nation-wide basis as a "normal" outcome of the process of growth and differentiation of the economy. Similarly, the rise to prominence within the firm of specialized executive functions is also a normal outcome of a process of growth in size and in structural differentiation. . . .

Generally speaking, Mills' argument is that the power of the very rich and the corporate rich *within* the economy is inordinately great and, by virtue of the factor of cumulative advantage, is becoming continually greater. At the very least, I think it can be said that his case is not proved and that there is equally good, if not better, evidence for an alternative view, particularly with reference to the trend.

First, I am not able to accept Mills' close identification of the very rich (i.e., the holders of "great fortunes") with the "corporate rich" (the primary holders of executive power in business organizations) as a single class in any very useful sense. Certainly, in the "heroic age" of American capitalism, from the Civil War to just after the turn of the century, the dominant figures were the entrepreneurs who, mainly as the founders of great enterprises and as the bankers and promoters concerned with mergers and reorganizations and the like, came to control these great organizations. But the dominant sociological fact of the outcome of that era was that these owning groups did not, as a group, succeed in consolidating their position precisely *within* their own enterprises and in the economy. It is a notorious fact that the *very* large enterprise still largely under family control through property holdings is much more the exception than the rule. Instead, the control has passed— by no means fully, but for the most part—to professional career executives, who have not reached their positions through the exercise of *property* rights but through some sort of process of appointment and promotion.

Mills concedes the main facts of this situation but fails, in my opinion, to evaluate them properly. It seems to be clear that the original "captains of industry," the makers of the great fortunes, *failed* to achieve or to exercise sufficient cumulative advantages to consolidate control of the enterprises in their families and their class ("class" in a sociological, not an economic, sense). This came about essentially because there were factors operating contrary to that of cumulative advantage, which Mills stresses so heavily. The main factor was the pressure to link executive responsibility with competence in such a way that the ascriptive rights of property ownership have tended to give way to the occupational functions of "professionals."

There are, above all, two ways in which Mills' treatment obscures the importance and nature of this shift. First, he continues to speak of power *within* the economy as based on property. To a considerable degree, of course, this is legally true, since the legal control of enterprise rests with stockholders. But, as Berle and Means first made abundantly clear, very generally it is not substantively true. In the old-style family enterprise, still predominant in the small-business sector of the economy, the functions of management and ownership are fused in the same people. In the larger enterprise they have by and large become differentiated. The fact that executives receive large salaries and bonuses is not to be twisted into an assumption that they control, so far as they do, through their property rights. Paradoxical as it may seem, a relatively backward industrial economy like that of France is far more *property*-based than is the case with the United States. In general, property holdings have not, of course, been expropriated, except for their diminution through inheritance and income taxes, which are not as negligible as Mills maintains. What has happened is that their relation to the *power* structure of the economy has been greatly altered. Mills almost entirely passes over this change.

The second problem concerns the process of recruitment in the higher occupational reaches of the economy. It is entirely clear that the process operates in the higher reaches overwhelmingly by appointment, i.e., the decisions of superiors as individuals or in small groups as to who should occupy certain positions. It is also true that the process is relatively unformalized—e.g., there are no competitive examinations and few, if any, formal qualifications of training. But from these facts Mills concludes, and again and again reiterates, that executive competence has very little, if anything, to do with the selection, that it is an overwhelmingly arbitrary process of choosing those who are congenial to the selectors, presumably because they can be counted upon to be "yes men." At the very least this contention is unproved, and I seriously doubt its correctness. There are certainly many difficulties and imperfections in the selection process. But I think it almost certain that

higher levels of competence are selected than would on the average
be the case through kinship ascription, and that, as such processes
go, the levels selected are relatively high.

One final point in this field. It does seem probable that the factor of cumulative advantage has a good deal to do with the high
levels of financial remuneration of the higher executive groups and
with the discrepancies between their incomes and those of governmental and professional people on comparable levels of competence
and responsibility. But this is very far from the great fortune level
of the founding entrepreneur type, and the evidence seems to be
that the discrepancy has not been cumulatively increasing to an
appreciable degree, particularly relative to wages at the labor levels;
cases like that of the academic profession are somewhat special.

So far I have been speaking about the nature and power position of the elite *within* the economy. The general tenor of my argument has been that, given the nature of an industrial society, a
relatively well-defined elite or leadership group *should be expected
to develop* in the business world; it is out of the question that
power should be diffused equally among an indefinite number of
very small units, as the ideal of pure competition and a good deal
of the ideology of business itself would have it. But first I question
whether the position of power of the business leadership groups
is such that a heavy operation of the factor of cumulative advantage must be invoked to account for it. Secondly, I must stress
that the business elite is no longer primarily an elite of *property*-
owners, but that its center of gravity has shifted to occupationally
professional executives or managers. Differential advantages of
family origin, etc., are about the same for admission to this group
as to other groups requiring educational and other qualifications.
Again the evidence is that the proportion of its members recruited
from the upper economic and social groups is and remains relatively high, but it has not, in recent times, been increasing, as the
theory of cumulative advantage would lead us to expect.

The problem of an elite within the economy must, however, be
clearly distinguished from that of an elite in the society as a whole
and the power position occupied by such an elite. There are two
main orders of questions bearing on the transition from one to the
other. Though a thorough consideration of this transition would
lead into very far-reaching questions, for present purposes one can
be treated rather briefly. Mills gives us the impression that "elite-
ness" in any society, including our own, is overwhelmingly a question

of the power that an individual or a group can command. By this, he means . . . influence on the "big" decisions directly affecting what happens in the society in the short run. But there are many elements in the society which are relatively powerless in this sense, but nevertheless of the greatest functional importance. Our society has almost divested kinship units as such of important power in this sense. But this does not mean at all that the family has ceased to be important. Closely linked with this is the question of the feminine role. Women qua women by and large do not have a position of power comparable to that of men; but this is not to say that they are unimportant—otherwise how can we account for the extent of our national preoccupations with questions of sexuality? Finally, there is a *distinct* difference between the rank-order of occupations—which, relative to other role-types, are closely involved with decision-making in a society like ours—by power and by prestige. The most striking case is the relatively high position of the professions relative to executive roles in business, as revealed by the famous North-Hatt data. Physicians as a group do not exercise great power, but there is no reason to question their very high prestige, which has been demonstrated in study after study.

The second main context, however, directly concerns the question of power. In a complex society the primary locus of power lies in the political system. . . . Two questions are . . . primary for our purposes: the degree of differentiation of the political system from other systems; and its own internal structure. These two problems, it will be noted, parallel those raised with reference to the economy.

For historical reasons it seems clear that the development of the American political system, since the breakdown of the first synthesis associated with the "founders of the Republic," has lagged behind that of the economy. This is a function primarily of the two factors already noted—the economic emphasis inherent in our system of values, and the relative lack of urgency of certain political problems because of our especially protected and favored national position. Relative to the economic structure, which had by that time grown enormously, the political was at its weakest in the period from the Civil War to the end of the century; this situation is sketched by Mills in broadly correct terms. Since then, both internal exigencies and the exigencies of our international position have been stimuli for major changes.

Internally, beyond the more elementary provisions for law and order and essential minimum services—much of this, of course, on a local basis—the main focus of the development of our political system has been *control* of economic organization and processes, and coping with some of the social consequences of economic growth and industrialization. The process started well before the turn of the century with the Interstate Commerce legislation and the Anti-Trust Act and continued through the New Deal era, not steadily but with waves of new measures and levels of political control.

A major problem in relation to Mills' analysis is whether this is "genuine" control. His view seems to be that at times it has been, but that on balance it is the business power-holders who control government, not vice versa; the above quotation about the outcome of the New Deal puts it succinctly. In my opinion this is a misinterpretation. If genuine and in some sense effective controls had not been imposed, I find it impossible to understand the bitter and continuing opposition on the part of business to the measures which have been taken. Even some of those most completely taken for granted now, like the Federal Reserve system, were bitterly fought at the time. It therefore seems to me to be the sounder interpretation that there has been a genuine growth of autonomous governmental power—apart from the military aspect, which will be discussed presently—and that one major aspect of this has been relatively effective control of the business system. This control and the growth of "big government" have been generally accepted in the society as a whole. The participation of big-business men in governmental processes is by no means to be interpreted as a simple index of their power to dominate government in their own interests, as Mills often seems to maintain.

To me, another indication of Mills' biased view of the governmental situation is his almost complete failure even to mention the political parties, or to analyze their differences. It seems to me broadly true that the Republican party, though a coalition, is more than any other single thing the party of the bigger sector of business. Four years of a Republican administration—two of them without control of Congress—is certainly not enough to indicate that big business through its favorite party organ controls the government on a long-run basis. So Mills is practically forced to the view that the alleged control operates above and beyond the party system. This seems to be connected with his relegation of the legislative branch to the "middle level" of power. I have strong reservations about this, but also it must not be forgotten that the presidency is the biggest prize of all in party politics, and it is its importance which forms the primary integrating focus of our particular type of party system. Surely the presidency is not simply the football of an inner clique which manipulates the executive branch independently of the party.

Mills, of course, recognizes that the aftermath of two world wars, the rise of Communist power, and the relative decline of the older Western Great Powers provide the occasion for the increasing prominence of the military group in our governmental system. Before these changes—and, indeed, to a remarkable extent, as late as the 1930's—the military played a far smaller role in this country than in any other society of comparable scale and organizational and technological development. Part of the change may be interpreted as simply the redressing of a balance. But it seems to me correct to say that for the last ten years there has been a special situation attributable to the extremely unsettled condition of the world at large and to the difficulties entailed for the American system, given its background, in meeting the problem on its own terms. There is thus a sense in which it is true that the higher military officers have tended to fill a vacuum in the field of national decision-making. There are two main points to be made about Mills' treatment of the matter. First, more in this field than perhaps any other, Mills' discussion is marred by a hasty tendency to generalize from very recent short-run developments to the long-run prospects of the structure of the society. Even here he fails to mention that in certain crucial questions the recommendations of the military have been overruled by civilian authority, although the President [Eisenhower] is a former military man. Secondly, the tone of indictment, particularly evidenced by the quite unnecessary and, I think, inappropriate parading of the term "warlord," is stronger in his discussion of this area than in any other, except perhaps the "mass society."

Related to the position of the higher military officers is what Mills calls the "military metaphysic," meaning the definition of international problems in terms of the primacy of military force. That there has been such a tendency, and that it has gone beyond the objective requirements of the situation, seem to be unquestionable. But I very much doubt whether it is as absolute as many of Mills' statements make it appear, and a swing in another direction is discernible already. This seems to be another case of Mills' tendency to make large generalizations about major trends from short-run experience.

Finally, let us say a word about what Mills calls the "political directorate"—that is, the non-military component in the groups most influential in the affairs of government and politics. Again I think there is a certain correctness in his contention that a definite weakness exists here, and that the high participation both of business and of military elements in the exercise of power is related to this. But a difficulty arises in terms of the perspective on American society which I have been emphasizing throughout. Both the non-political stress in American social structure and values generally, and the recency and intensity of the pressures to build up this aspect of our structure, would lead one to predict that it would be a major focus of strain. American society has not developed a well-integrated political-government elite, in the sense that it has developed a relatively well-integrated business-executive group. For this reason responsibility has been carried—imperfectly, of course—by a very miscellaneous group which includes members of the business and military groups, as would be expected, but also "politicians," in the usual sense of people making an at least partial career out of elective office and the influencing of elections; professional people, particularly lawyers but also economists, political scientists, and even natural scientists (e.g., John von Neumann as Atomic Energy Commissioner); journalists; and, a very important element, upper-class people in more than the purely economic sense that Mills employs, of whom Franklin Roosevelt was one and Adlai Stevenson, though also a lawyer, is another. In my opinion, the structure of the American political leadership group is far from a settled thing. It certainly is not settled in terms of the long-run dominance of a business-military coalition.

Mills holds that the United States has no higher civil service at all, in the European sense, and seems to imply that we should have. There is relative truth in his empirical contention, though I think he tends to underestimate the real influence of "non-political" government officials on longer-run policy. At least it seems highly probable that in the nature of the case the tendency will be toward a strengthening of the element of professional governmental officials who are essentially independent both of short-run "politics" and of elements extraneous to the structure of government and its responsibilities. In fact, the military officer is a special case of this type, and though his role is not stabilized, it presumably must come to be more important than it traditionally has been. However, it is questionable how far the specific models of civil service organization either of Britain or of Continental Europe—particularly, certain of their special connections with the class structure and the educational system—are appropriate to American conditions. Such connections in the American case would accentuate rather than mitigate the prominence of the Ivy League element to which Mills so seriously objects.

Above all, I do not think that Mills has made a convincing case for his contention that the power structure impinging directly on American government is in process of crystallizing into a top business-military coalition with a much weaker political "junior partner" whose main function presumably is, by manipulation of the mass media and the political process in the narrower sense, to keep the great majority of Americans from protesting too loudly or even from awakening to what allegedly is "really" going on. On a number of counts which have been reviewed, there is a case on a short-run basis for part of his interpretation. But I think that the kinds of factors brought out in the previous discussion make it extremely dubious that even the partial correctness of his interpretation of a current situation will prove to be a sound indicator of what is to be expected over such longer periods as a generation or more.

My conviction on this point is strengthened by a variety of other considerations which, for reasons of space, cannot be discussed here, but may be mentioned. First, I am extremely skeptical of Mills' interpretation of what he calls the "mass society," which includes the structural position of the great majority of the American population. In this he ignores both kinship and friendship, and the whole mass of associational activities and relationships. One example is the spread of church membership—which I suppose Mills would dismiss as simply an escape from the boredom of white-collar life, but in my opinion is of considerable positive significance.

Another very important complex which Mills either treats cavalierly or ignores completely involves education at the various levels, and with it the enormous development, over a century, of science and learning and the professions resting upon them. It is true that the people rooted in these areas of the social structure are not prominent in the power elite, and are even subject to some conflicts with it; but they would not be expected to be prominent in this way—their functions in the society are different. Nonetheless, they must be taken very seriously into account in a diagnosis of what has been happening to the society as a whole. One of the most important sets of facts concerns the ways in which the services of technical professional groups have come to penetrate the structures both of business and of government, a circumstance which over a period of time has greatly enhanced the role of the universities as custodians of learning and sources of trained personnel.

Finally, there is one special case of a professional group whose role Mills treats with serious inadequacy—namely, lawyers. First, he dismisses the judicial branch of government as just "trailing along," with the implication that with a slight lag it simply does the bidding of the "real" holders of power. This seems to be a most biased appraisal of the role of the courts. Not to speak of the longer-run record, the initiative taken by the courts in the matter of racial segregation and in the reassertion of civil liberties after the miasma of McCarthyism does not appear to me to be compatible with Mills' views. Similar considerations seem to apply to various aspects of the role of the private legal profession, notably with respect to the *control* of processes in the business world. Mills tends to assume that the relation between law and business is an overwhelmingly one-way relation; lawyers are there to serve the interests of businessmen and essentially have no independent influence. This, I think, is an illusion stemming largely from Mills' preoccupation with a certain kind of power. His implicit reasoning seems to be that since lawyers have less power than businessmen, they do not really "count."

Suggestions for Further Reading

Some of the more penetrating interpretations of American political life have been produced by foreign observers. Although Tocqueville here stands surrogate for them all, one other classic of this kind must be mentioned: Lord Bryce, *The American Commonwealth* (New York, 1888, 2 vols.), conveniently accessible in an abridged paper-back edition (New York, 1959), with an introduction by Louis Hacker. (The student may wish to compare Bryce's impression of the "uniformity of American life" in vol. II, part VI, ch. 11, with the assumption of some contemporary pluralists of its "frightening diversity.") A rich selection from the foreign traveler literature is Oscar Handlin, *This Was America* (Cambridge, 1949).

Daniel Boorstin's approach is further elaborated in his major work in progress, *The Americans,* vol. I: *The Colonial Experience* (New York, 1958) and vol. II: *The National Experience* (New York, 1965). In *The Founding of New Societies* (New York, 1964), Louis Hartz builds on his earlier analysis of America as an archetypal nonfeudal society—*The Liberal Tradition in America* (New York, 1955)—to present a more general theory concerning five societies (Australia, Canada, Latin America, South Africa, and the United States) created by European migration. In each of these societies, Hartz explains, an ideological and social fragment detached itself from the larger whole of Europe to become the whole of a new nation. In these terms three centuries of American political experience can be traced to the original extrication of a bourgeois-liberal fragment from the turmoil of seventeenth-century England. See also Hartz's essay "Rise of the Democratic Idea" in *Paths of American Thought,* ed. A. M. Schlesinger, Jr. and Morton White (Boston, 1963), pp. 37–51.

A number of critiques of Boorstin's and Hartz's views are available. A considerably modified version of his earlier treatment of the cult of consensus is found in John Higham, *History* (Englewood Cliffs, N.J., 1965), pp. 212–232. In *Equality and Liberty* (New York, 1965), pp. 3–41, 114–139, Harry V. Jaffa discusses Boorstin and the consensual theory of American politics. A symposium on Hartz is all too briefly summarized by Charles G. Sellers in the *Mississippi Valley Historical Review,* XLIX (September, 1962), 292-293. Participants were Marvin Meyers, Harry V. Jaffa, Leonard Krieger, and Louis Hartz. Neal Riemer, in *The Democratic Experiment* (Princeton, N.J., 1967), argues that American democracy cannot be understood merely as the automatic unfolding of an English liberal fragment or an automatic response to a favorable American environment. Rather, he maintains, creative Americans selected and rejected from their Old World inheritance, adapted to and took advantage of their New World environment, and responded—often with great imagination and wisdom—to the sometimes unique problems that faced them. See also Riemer's critique of Boorstin, "Two Conceptions of the Genius of American Politics," *Journal of Politics,* XX (November, 1958), 695-717. William J. Newman's *Futilitarian Society* (New York, 1961) is a visceral reaction to the presumed conservative implications of Boorstin's and Hartz's work.

The view that consensus has been achieved or preserved repeatedly in American political history by compromises at the expense of Negro interests and rights might be styled, perhaps sardonically, the "Negro interpretation of American politics." C. Vann Woodward, in *Reunion and Reaction: The Compromise of 1877 and the End of Reconstruction* (Boston, 1951) describes one such major compromise at the dawn of the modern era of American politics. A fascinating chapter on "The American Oppositions" in Robert Dahl, ed., *Political Oppositions in Western Democracies* (New Haven, 1966) extends the implications of the historical analyses of Woodward and his colleagues. Here Dahl maintains that the "ancient issue of Negro rights" has held the "central (if not always public) place in politics," and that the one condition above all which created the pattern of cleavages dominating American politics was "the power of the one-party South in elections and in Congress and its virtually unbreakable unity on the institutions of white supremacy in the South." At the time of writing Dahl appeared rather hopeful that this "ancient issue" would soon no longer be central to our politics; his expectation was that American politics might then regroup itself along lines of greater programmatic and ideological consistency.

Two collections of essays are primary sources on the frontier thesis: Frederick Jackson Turner, *The Frontier in American History* (New York, 1920) and *The Significance of Sections in American*

History (New York, 1932). A selection has been made by Ray Allen Billington, *Frontier and Section* (Englewood Cliffs, N.J., 1961), and two important critical assessments of Turner are G. W. Pierson, "The Frontier and American Institutions," *New England Quarterly,* XV (June, 1942), 224–255, and Benjamin F. Wright, "American Democracy and the Frontier," *Yale Review* XX (December, 1930), 349–365. A useful collection of articles—pro and con—is in George R. Taylor, ed., *The Turner Thesis* (Boston, 1956). For an exhaustive bibliography of the literature on every aspect of the subject see Ray Allen Billington, *The Frontier Heritage* (New York, 1966).

It has usually been assumed that Turner developed his frontier thesis in reaction to the "germ theory" of a late nineteenth-century generation of scholars, exemplified by Herbert Baxter Adams, *The Germanic Origins of New England Towns,* (Baltimore, 1882) and Woodrow Wilson, *The State* (Boston, 1884). In the period when Turner was serving his apprenticeship as a historian, the orthodox social scientists affirmed that innate racial traits determined a people's political destiny. Herbert Baxter Adams taught that American political institutions merely reproduced those which the Germanic race had long before evolved in the Teutonic forests. On the other hand, Gilman M. Ostrander in his essay "Turner and the Germ Theory," *Journal of Agricultural History,* XXXII (October, 1958), 258–261, points out that Turner's environmentalism was based on an implicit racial inheritance premise. According to Ostrander, Turner always assumed that the frontier worked its magic so effectively because it brought out the inherent biological superiorities of at least some of the nation's settlers. Thomas Jefferson, an exponent of an even earlier version of this kind of inheritance theory, held that American democracy represented a purer form of those Saxon institutions which in the home country had been deformed by the Norman Conquest. See, for example, Jefferson's letter to John Cartwright, June 4, 1824, in *Writings of Thomas Jefferson,* ed. Andrew A. Lipscomb and Albert E. Bergh (Washington, D.C., 1905), XVI, 42–52.

Major works setting forth the Progressive interpretation of American politics are J. Allen Smith, *The Spirit of American Government* (New York, 1907); Charles A. and Mary Beard, *The Rise of American Civilization* (New York, 1927); and Vernon Louis Parrington, *Main Currents in American Thought* (New York, 1927–1930). An impressive restatement, along Neo-Progressive and undogmatic Marxist lines, of the economic and social class determination of

American politics is Barrington Moore, *Social Origins of Dictator-ship and Democracy* (Boston, 1966), pp. 111–155. For Moore the Civil War was the last great capitalist offensive; its outcome re-shaped modern American democracy.

The interpretation of American politics that prevails in the Com-munist world is well represented in Alan F. Westin, ed., *Views of America* (New York, 1966). For Communist writers, American poli-tics is a facade behind which lurks the decisive power of the "great monopolies." A recent interpretation by American Marxists is Paul A. Baran and Paul M. Sweezy, *Monopoly Capital: An Essay on the American Economic and Social Order* (New York, 1966). See also the essay by Howard L. Parsons in Herbert Aptheker, ed., *Marx-ism and Democracy* (New York, 1965). An important book by a British Marxist, summing up a lifetime of study of American insti-tutions, is Harold Laski, *The American Democracy* (New York, 1948). William Appleman Williams, *The Tragedy of American Diplomacy* (Cleveland, 1959) and *The Great Evasion* (Chicago, 1964), espouses a point of view much in vogue among adherents of the New Left. Williams argues in Marxist terms that American politics is best understood as capitalist and imperialist politics. In his analysis, American politicians have followed in the twentieth century a policy of indefinite extension of American political, eco-nomic, and cultural influence, because they view ever-enlarging foreign markets as necessary to the survival of the capitalist eco-nomic order. In *The Contours of American History* (Cleveland, 1961), Williams describes American politics as an arena of struggle between the forces of community-mindedness and rampant indi-vidualism. Socialist perspectives on American politics are found in Gabriel Kolko, *Wealth and Power in America* (New York, 1962) and in Michael Harrington, *The Other America* (New York, 1964).

Much of the debate on the relevance of American political expe-rience to others has centered on the meaning of the American Revolution. Richard B. Morris in *The American Revolution Recon-sidered* (New York, 1967) affirms the pertinence of the Revolution to our own "Neo-Revolutionary era." He also considers oversimple the view that America "skipped" the feudal stage of history. Bernard Keiran, "Limitations of United States Policy Toward the Underdeveloped World," *American Scholar*, XXXI (Spring, 1962), 208–219, feels that Americans have difficulty in comprehending national revolutions to reorder society because America's experi-ence of revolution is limited. See also Edward Handler, *America and Europe in the Political Thought of John Adams* (Cambridge, 1964). R. R. Palmer, *Age of the Democratic Revolution* (Princeton, N.J., 1959-1964, 2 vols.), especially II, 509-543, concludes that there is no real parallel between the problems of the United States in the 1790's and those of the new nations today. But he also warns against exaggerations of American uniqueness, placing the American Revolution in the larger context of a general Western revolutionary agitation in the late eighteenth century. William N. Chambers, *Political Parties in a New Nation* (New York, 1963), like Lipset, maintains that study of the political experience of the United States may assist today's new nations in the search for answers to their own problems of political development.

Robert Dahl's pluralist view of American politics is elaborated in four books: with Charles E. Lindblom, *Politics, Economics and Welfare* (New York, 1953); *A Preface to Democratic Theory* (Chicago, 1956); *Who Governs?* (New Haven, 1961); and *Pluralist Democracy in the United States* (Chicago, 1967). Other pluralist analyses are found in David Riesman, *The Lonely Crowd* (New Haven, 1950), Ch. 10, and J. K. Galbraith, *American Capitalism* (Boston, 1956). See also David Truman, *The Governmental Process* (New York, 1951); Earl Latham, *The Group Basis of Politics* (Ithaca, 1952); and Arthur F. Bentley, *The Process of Government* (Chicago, 1908), a classic of American political science neglected until recently.

One current trend in political science is to express serious reservations about some of the consequences of American pluralist politics. Representative are Grant McConnell, *Private Power and American Democracy* (New York, 1966); Theodore Lowi, "The Public Philosophy: Interest Group Liberalism," *American Political Science Review,* LXI (March, 1967), 5-24; and Henry S. Kariel, "The Body Politic and the Promise of a New Diagnostic," *Social Research,* XXXIV (Summer, 1967), 303-321.

A good statement of the Neo-Calhounite interpretation appears in Peter Drucker, "A Key to American Politics: Calhoun's Pluralism," *The Review of Politics,* X (October, 1948), 412-426. For the principle of the concurrent majority as originally proposed, see John C. Calhoun, *A Disquisition on Government,* ed. with an introduction by C. Gordon Post (Indianapolis, 1953).

Contemporary statements of the elite dominance position are C. Wright Mills, *The Power Elite* (New York, 1956); Floyd Hunter, *Top Leadership, U.S.A.* (Chapel Hill, 1953); and G. William Domhoff, *Who Rules America?* (Englewood Cliffs, N.J., 1967). The student may wish to look up Dwight D. Eisenhower's Farewell Speech, reprinted in the *New York Times,* January 18, 1964, warning against dangers of possible capture of public policy by an "industrial-military complex" or a "scientific-technological elite." Critical discussions of Mills's views abound and continue to multiply. Among them are Robert A. Dahl, "A Critique of the Ruling Elite Model," *American Political Science Review,* LII (June, 1958), 463–469; Daniel Bell, *End of Ideology* (New York, 1961), pp. 47–74; John H. Bunzel, *Anti-Politics in America* (New York, 1967), pp. 91–112; and Arnold M. Rose, *The Power Structure* (New York, 1967). Mills made a lively reply to some of his critics in *Dissent,* V (Winter, 1957), 22–34. An original analysis of the strengths and weaknesses of both the pluralist and elite dominance approaches is Theodore Lowi's review article in *World Politics,* XVI (July, 1964), 677–715. See also Peter Bachrach and Morton Baratz, "Two Faces of Power," *American Political Science Review,* LVI (December, 1962), 947–952; and Shin'ya Ono, "The Limits of Bourgeois Pluralism," *Studies on the Left,* V (Winter, 1965), 46–72.

After his confrontation with a perhaps bewildering variety of conflicting interpretations, the student may find refreshing the viewpoint of the already cited book by Daniel Bell that American political reality is too diverse and complex to be subsumed under any single theory.